M000201087

To Kat

A little gift from across the pond.

I love you more than anything - even Mealiquor

Love Rhys xxx

The MEATliquor Chronicles
Chapter and Verse

The MEATliquor Chronicles
Chapter and Verse

YIANNI PAPOUTSIS and **SCOTT COLLINS**

Aided and Abetted by
DBC PIERRE and **GILES LOOKER**

FABER & FABER

✝

CONTENTS

✝

DISCLAIMER

GOD IS BUSY

I'M AS close as you'll get. Anyhow, a damned child could see that no responsibility will be taken by anyone for a single word in here. It's just plain irresponsible. Nothing I see does service to anything, all it does is degrade the proper order of things. They say beauty is strange in its proportions but this is just damned bizarre and I wash my hands of it. If you die from any shit in here, don't come crying to me.

Alfonso, Wingman of God

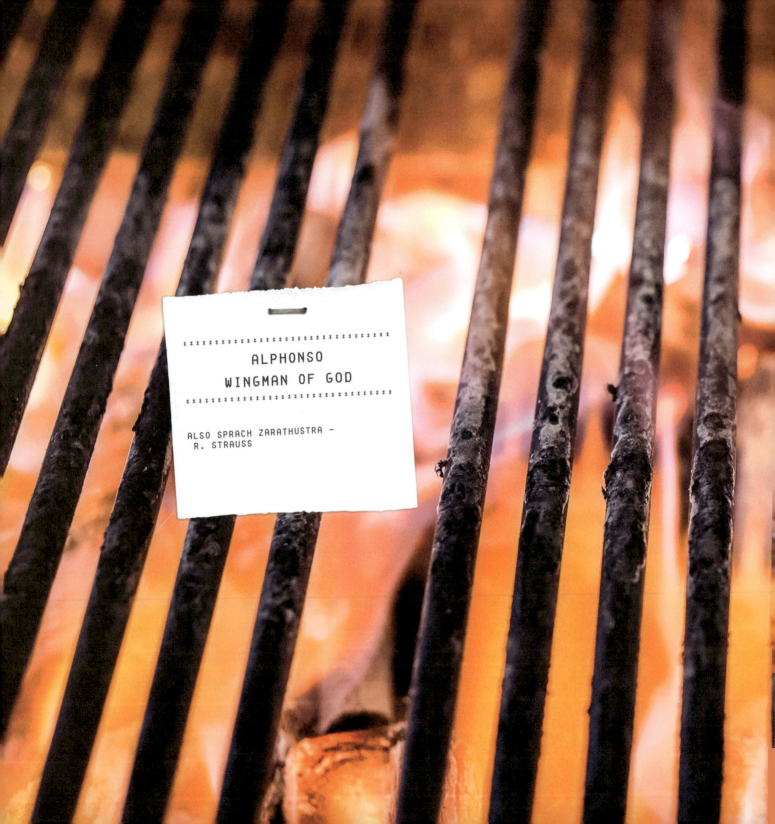

THE PRECARNAL PERIOD

LIGHT

THE MEATliquor CHRONICLES
PART ONE

666 words (mark of the Beast)

It keep me with ramblin' mind, rider
Every old place I go, every old place I go
I can tell, the wind is risin'.

The leaves tremblin' on the tree,
Tremblin' on the tree,
I can tell, the wind is risin',
Leaves tremblin' on the tree.

HONEY and brimstone boil inside some people; it's a combustion of extremes that powers souls, getting vaporous, hot, expansive, spilling too close to freedom and death at once. The only way to cool the crucible is to vent it before it explodes; and at midnight in the right mix of light, dark, chaos, mischief and calm, that's what the folk in this book will be doing, all together in different places. If you can identify with it, the idea of eroding shit before it corrodes you, read on. All myths arise from that spirit, and are born as truths. They are the gas of flying moments, blown when our present, still glowing, becomes a past. Those presents are what stay in us, and this book is their chronicle and recipe. Going to town may never be the same.

On Sunday 20th of June 1937, on the third floor at 508 Park Avenue in Dallas, Texas, just such a flying moment tied four people symbolically to the idea of this book. Each will tell his story; I'm the fourth one and will paint the back story that ties us to you.

You are now the fifth one.

Sure, meat and liquor live on these pages, but let's be clear: what we celebrate is a spirit, one that's gaining power, and better yet, one that goes against our day.

And good, because our day is shit.

If you've ever waited hours to get into a gig, you'll have an inkling of where this is headed; either way we aim to show why we gather like moths around a flame, or at least explain the flame – and why we should keep gathering. It will involve reversing a pre-Christian legend, but you know it won't be the first legend we had to fuck with to find our place in the world.

So all in good time. For now, because the best things unfold at the speed of hard ice, go and find the best ice, fix a drink and turn your mind to the notion of Quality, because that's where we're aiming – not quality as in sofa advertising, but Quality as Pirsig has it: of life at its rudest, the unrepentant Quality of organisms throbbing towards the good. In line with that, how wrong would it feel to explore these gospels through any kind of e-shit? Perhaps because ideas have weight. People have weight, life has weight, experiences have weight – a book has weight. So we meet in a book. It's correct. Nobody can like or dislike us. They can tweet it out their ass. This book is an end in itself. It never needs upgrading. It doesn't self-lock. You agree no terms to buy it. You untick no box, open no account, sign no contract, receive no mail, reveal no whereabouts. Nobody will come in a year's time to make you pay for it again. It is a universe which you carry in your hand and open at the speed of your nature, again and again, for ever. It belongs only to you and is under your control. It promises no happiness, identifies no problem in you. It has a smell, a texture, a colour, a style, and three organic dimensions. It teaches of, and for, and against all the things you choose it to, and is a human right whose loss would be an end to freedom. Because once every battery is in enemy hands, and all our little screens are dead – it will speak for you a thousand years more, and wear your stains upon it.

Stain the book. Cook the food, drink the drinks. If you're still standing by the end, come find us.

Our mission will have barely begun.

DBC

✟

YIANNI PAPOUTSIS

MISANTHROPE. PHILANTHROPIST

999 words (the Beast after burgers)
As told to DBC Pierre

EVEN once we accept that people are not born equal, that a conspiracy of breeding and chance primes the pump of a man's constitution – the question of Yianni Papoutsis rankles on. Science, still arguing over why men even have nipples, hasn't imagined a graph or algorithm to describe him; so for this biography we resort to slander, speculation and lies. It's all we can do, when Papoutsis will only say he's from South London, and even the most credible sightings describe him as 'a fackin blur'.

Let's whittle the question down: we know he exists because you and I woke up grateful for milk. Therefore all the stories, from Constantinople to Herng Gong and Hamburg, must be true, all have that gratitude in common. So we're dealing with a traveller of considerable range and impact, a perpetual one, whose natural territory expands with his footfall. Of all the tales we have to sift through, one says that he carries a stick of chalk in his back pocket, that wherever he lies down he draws a room around himself. But we can't confirm this without going into his pocket or lying down with him, so it will stay unconfirmed – anyway, to me it sounds too much like Italian opera.

And that's where things get interesting: Papoutsis has actually been seen around opera and theatre, not once but again and again, over years, in numerous countries, and was even seen running with packs of actors and minstrels.

Ask yourself – do the words Opera and Peckham go together? No. Something else is going on. We can have an educated stab at it by following this clue: among reports from his theatre days, many describe Papoutsis's uncanny ability with theatre rigging. One witness even described him as 'a fackin monkey' – although that could just have been how much Papoutsis owed him. Still: opera, theatre rigging, are these the tastes and skills of a Peckham lad? No; but could they be the tastes and skills of a scorned heir to a vast Greek shipping fortune, disowned and raised on steamships?

Very possibly. One tale persists which puts our clues into context: it says that the young Papoutsis was raised by Palikari – Greek Partisans – in the bilges and rigging of merchant ships; that below-decks was his domain, that he smuggled choice cuts from west to east and back again, that if he hadn't been found running a brothel and souvlaki joint above a prop-shaft, he might still be there today.

But he's not. How do we know?

The sale on eBay of the title '16th in line to the Greek throne' tells us so. Yianni Papoutsis cashed those 400 drachma and vanished into the Nevada Desert for what have been described as some 'fackin dark' years, running with showgirls, pimps, hustlers and banjo players. He'd sold his heritage.

From there he didn't surface until 2009 – the first recorded sighting of him in Peckham, captaining that most elusive and infamous burger van, the MEATwagon. It was as if an occult hand had plucked him from one life to another. As Papoutsis grew more visible it became clear that his passion for meat was matched only by his love of illegal warehouse parties and strobe lighting; finding these complementary he began to host illicit 'meatings' in car parks and industrial estates all over London, calling the faithful on Japanese war drums. Except for one unfortunate sighting of Prince Philip and Queen Sofía at a windswept Catford meating, his true background had been erased by 2010.

But one's inner past is not so easily discarded; Yianni's sympathy for shipping and mayhem were soon being expressed via the infamous Towpath Festivals, held on abandoned wastegrounds along London's canals. Hundreds of revellers descended to eat, drink and dance into the smallest hours; but for a glimpse of King Constantine, and a sticky situation with a barge, they might all still be there. Papoutsis's call to the faithless, however, made him too

visible; a black sheep is missed most by those he made whiter, and those old forces massed against him, first vandalising, then stealing two MEATwagons within a year. Still he refused to acknowledge the right of intelligence services to meddle in his affairs, and in 2011 mounted a counter offensive by teaming up with Scott Collins. It wasn't that Collins ran the pubs where the intelligence services drank – but he ran the pubs where their women drank, often secretly.

Enemies vanished. The Promised Land shone ahead.

Papoutsis brought the shadowy Giles Looker into the conspiracy, and on 11.01.11 opened #MEATEASY, the mythical burger joint and cocktail bar where night-time never ended. Located above a crack-house and below a brothel in New Cross, #MEATEASY took London by storm for the brief period it lived, with pilgrims queuing for up to three hours to worship. Rumour has it a real Hellhound guarded the door. In the summer of 2011 Papoutsis unleashed a third MEATwagon on the public, the customised Chevrolet ambulance known as 'Florence', and has spent summers since with his Hellhound crew, taunting authorities and causing debauch at festivals and so-called 'private events' all over the UK. His contribution to a street-food renaissance won him the inaugural 2010 British Street Food Awards at the Ludlow Food Festival, where he bribed his way onto the judging panel. He has since appeared on screen, online, on radio and in print, nationally and internationally, but says this was the work of impostors as he can only write Cyrillic.

In the end we can only know the truth about deeply rooted men, men whose fruits grow year upon year in one place. But Papoutsis is like Black Rock City; his roots are his feet, and just as quickly as he constitutes to full force on the spot where he stands, he can be gone without a trace. Perhaps it's no coincidence that most persistent sightings of him were at Black Rock City. We know they're credible.

They all describe him as 'a fackin blur'.

SPAG BOL

AS BRITISH as Chicken Tikka Masala and the Doner Kebab, Spag Bol defines the essence of traditional British fayre in that, like all our best dishes, it was originally nicked from Johnny Foreigner (traditionally at gunpoint) then bent to our collective palate in our kitchens when we got home.

Although nowadays it's often served as a form of modern-day gruel in institutions such as schools, prisons and asylums, it can nevertheless be a magnificent and hearty dish when prepared with a bit of TLC. It's the definition of comfort food (especially with peas). For me, in many ways, it transcends the Italian original.

This is a personal dish, designed to be played around with and tuned to your own taste: some people prefer it more tomatoey, some more beefy; some prefer chunky, some smooth; some like it wet and sloppy, others dry and meaty.

Always use whole canned tomatoes rather than chopped – they're generally much better-quality tomatoes and they seem to be less acidic.

YP

WHAT YOU NEED

Serves 4

400g beef mince
1 tbsp tomato paste
1 can whole plum tomatoes
1 large carrot, diced
1 large onion, minced
3 cloves garlic, minced

A couple of bay leaves
½ tsp oregano
½ tsp thyme
Salt and pepper
200ml beef stock
A bottle of red wine
A splash of milk
A squirt of ketchup
A pinch of chilli powder
A handful of frozen petits pois
Worcestershire sauce
Grated mozzarella and cheddar
Parmesan
Dried spaghetti

WHAT YOU DO

In a heavy pan over a very high heat, brown the meat in small batches – it needs to be properly brown, not grey and boiled.

Remove the meat from the pan, set aside and turn down the heat.

Add the carrots and onions and cook very slowly until they start to colour. Add the garlic and continue to cook for a minute.

Add the meat back into the pan together with the tomato paste and stir well for a couple of minutes.

Add the tinned tomatoes and mash/chop them until they're only slightly chunky.

Let it cook down, covered, over a very low heat for half an hour.

Add the stock and the red wine slowly. Add herbs, chilli, ketchup and a splash of Worcestershire sauce.

Add the peas and let it cook for another 15 minutes or so then add the milk and a small squirt of tomato ketchup if the sauce is still too acidic.

Take time to balance the flavours and allow them to amalgamate slowly – they will develop during cooking. Ideally let it sit off the heat for 20 minutes before serving while you cook the spaghetti.

Use a big pan full of a lot of very salted water. Bring to a rolling boil then add your spaghetti. Cover immediately and cook it until *al dente*.

Drain and toss the spaghetti in a pan with a little of the sauce to coat the strands then top with more sauce when you plate up.

Cover with the grated mozzarella and cheddar with a touch of grated Parmesan.

Bang it under the grill for a couple of minutes until the cheese has melted and begun to brown.

Drink: a big fuck-off Italian red – a Barolo or an Amarone.

PAN CON TOMATE

A.K.A. AN ANARCHIST'S BREAKFAST

IN THE fertile valleys of Granada old men still rouse their mules at dawn to tend their crops of tomatoes, olives, almonds and weed. Acequias, stone channels cut into the mountainsides by the Romans and the Moors, still bring snowmelt from the peaks to irrigate the terraces exactly as they have done for the past two thousand years.

A half-hour's drive to the south, in the desert of Almeria, is one of the most surreal places in Western Europe. An otherworldly shantytown where the white tarps of the plasticulture tents, known locally as 'plasticos', stretch as far as the eye can see, merging into the sea and the sky. It's estimated that they cover 20,000 hectares, an area equivalent to 45,000 football fields. In dusty alleyways between high, white, plastic walls, the ragged strips of the abandoned plasticos flutter in the breeze and drift across the road like some toxic, twenty-first-century iteration of the tumbleweed that used to blow across screen in the Spaghetti Westerns filmed a hundred or so miles away in Little Hollywood.

This is a place of race riots, of murders, of drugs, of people-smuggling. This is a place of terrible poverty. The workers, mostly illegal immigrants – originally from North Africa, but more often of Eastern European origin nowadays – stumble along the dust tracks, their eyes dead and staring from a combination of heatstroke, the effects of the chemicals they pump into those tents, and the chemicals they pump into themselves. They exist in overcrowded shacks made from scavenged pallets and corrugated plastic sheets.

They grow tomatoes in there. Insipid, watery and tasteless tomatoes. They ship most of them to the UK.

YP

WHAT YOU NEED

Like many of the best dishes in the world it is one of the simplest, showcasing and highlighting the ingredients.

Bread, ideally a day-old baguette
Tomatoes
Sea salt
Black pepper
Garlic cloves
EVOO (extra-virgin olive oil)

WHAT YOU DO

Cut the tomatoes into smallish chunks and place in a sieve. Toss them with a bit of salt and let them sit for half an hour. A pale pink liquid will ooze out. This is tasteless and can be thrown away. The remaining tomatoes will have a much more intense flavour.

Using a stick blender, pulse the tomatoes quickly with a couple of drops of EVOO until you have a slightly lumpy paste. Add a pinch of sugar and/or a drop of lemon juice if necessary.

Toast the bread and rub a couple of peeled garlic cloves over one side to flavour it.

Spread the tomato paste on the bread and top with a few drops of EVOO. Add salt and pepper to taste.

Serve with jamón curado or Manchego.

Drink: Sol y Sombra (equal parts anisette and brandy).

GREEK LEMON CHICKEN

THE GREEK

Hosted by Torgren Torgrensson

AN OLD Icelandic children's rhyme tells us all we need to know about this creature: 'That'll be three pounds. Have you got anything smaller?'

Actually, perhaps not a rhyme, but something heard in the dens where this most gay and colourful race gathers to make their fearsome din. I was hesitant to visit such a den at first as I saw a man wearing a dress at the door; once inside I could scarcely believe my eyes as the party quickly alternated between gaiety and rage, one moment dancing, the next smashing crockery. The Greek will drink a strong and fragrant liquor which is much to my taste, and is doubtless a reason why I cannot remember more to tell. Except that I awoke broke and with ringing ears.

It is reliably said that only an Armenian is a match for this most wily of races; perhaps this accounts for their having infiltrated the major royal families of the world, passing seemingly unnoticed, although the smell of their food is said to haunt most palaces.

My advice: make an excuse if approached by one, and watch from a safe distance.

WHAT YOU NEED

Serves 3–4

100g butter, softened
50g butter, melted
100ml olive oil
1 chicken
6 roasting potatoes, peeled and cut into wedges
5 cloves garlic, minced
2 unwaxed lemons
1 tbsp dried oregano (preferably Greek)
½ tsp dried rosemary
Salt and pepper
½ pint chicken stock
A glass of white wine
Zest of half a lemon

WHAT YOU DO

Using your fingers, gently smear the butter between the skin and the flesh of the chicken, being careful not to split the skin.

Juice both lemons and insert the skins into the chicken's cavity. Rub the outside of the chicken with salt and refrigerate for 20 minutes.

In a baking tray arrange the potatoes around the chicken (breast down). Mix half the melted butter with the olive oil, white wine, chicken stock, garlic and lemon juice, and pour over the chicken and potatoes. Sprinkle with salt, pepper, rosemary and oregano.

Cook at 180 °C in a preheated oven for 40 minutes. Turn the chicken over, breast-side up, baste everything well and cook for a further 10 minutes until tender and golden, adding more of the liquid as required. Sprinkle the lemon zest over everything 5 minutes before the end of cooking.

Let the chicken rest for 10 minutes, then just before serving pour the remaining hot melted butter over the chicken skin.

Serve with: steamed dandelions or spinach drenched in lemon juice.

SCALOPPINI DI VITELLO AL MARSALA

FOODS OF ITALY

Hosted by Torgren Torgrensson

MUCH like its people, the food of Italy tends to be short and swarthy, and involve heavily flavoured coatings to disguise blandness. One possible exception to this is the recipe they call Scaloppini, a dish of faux-horse which is known to halt shouting and gesticulating among local people, making it much prized for its very necessary calmative properties.

As biology teaches us, every young cow passes through a stage of being a horse, and in this stage is most tender and full of life-giving adrenaline. If you doubt it, look at humans in the womb – all pass through a stage of being a man before some are struck unlucky. In this stage the young horse is completely white and its meats are devoid of fibres, making it the most succulent of horses to eat, or indeed even to play with, in a certain way.

Damn. My wife has glimpsed this writing and run to her mother's with a suitcase. While I deal with her, here is a recipe for tender young horse, as perfectly remembered by a lad in his own foal days of life.

Behind an opera house with my parents in Rome.

I remember playing Gauntlet in the departure lounge at Gatwick while we waited to board, so I guess we're talking around 1986.

Late. Raining. Hungry. Wet.

The stage-door restaurant offered food, wine and warmth, and also a proprietor who started out drunk and ended up … Drunk.

Pouring my parents' wine from a barrel, he filled two glasses, knocked them both back standing right there in front of us, refilled the same glasses he'd just drunk from and took them to another table.

He didn't take a food order; he just brought us what he thought we'd want. That was how I tried, and fell in love with, this dish.

He also introduced me to Amaro Averna that night. A love affair that continues to this day.

Years later, on tour around the North of England, a world away from the grandeur of Italy, behind another opera house I found somewhere that recreated this dish exactly as I remembered it.

Seeking shelter from the rain and misery that defines Stoke-on-Trent, my desperate colleagues and I happened upon an Italian restaurant straight out of the 1970s: all wicker-wrapped carafes and plastic gingham tablecloths.

Cowering among the urban decay that festers around the bus station, our little Italian served the worst wine but the best veal I have ever tasted. Tender, succulent young meat in a rich, velvety sauce …

Sadly, the restaurant is no longer there.

It was probably stolen.

As with so many of my recipes, this is another one constructed from sensory memories. It's a perfect dish for a romantic dinner for two.

Ask your butcher to cut the escalopes thin.

If you're a vegetarian, you can also do this with chicken instead of veal.

YP

WHAT YOU NEED

Serves 2

100g plain flour
½ tsp salt
½ tsp finely ground black pepper
½ tsp white pepper
½ tsp garlic powder
½ tsp paprika
Milk
1 egg
2 veal escalopes
2 cloves garlic, finely minced
1 small onion, thinly sliced
100g chestnut or small portobello mushrooms, sliced
3 tsp olive oil for frying
50ml and a splash of Marsala wine
100ml chicken stock
1 tsp balsamic vinegar
30g butter
30ml double cream
Small bunch fresh parsley, chopped

WHAT YOU DO

Wrap the scaloppini in clingfilm or a Ziploc bag.

Pound them thin – ideally with a meat hammer, but you can also use a rolling pin, cricket bat or your fist (be aware they're going to double in size and take care not to get too into it and completely destroy the texture of the meat).

Mix the flour, salt, pepper, white pepper, garlic powder and paprika in a large bowl.

Mix the egg and milk into a very thin egg-wash.

Dredge the scaloppini in the seasoned flour, then the egg-wash, then the seasoned flour again. Set aside.

Fry the onions and mushrooms in olive oil until just starting to colour. Add half the butter and the garlic and fry over a medium heat, being careful not to let the garlic burn.

Shake off any excess flour and add the scaloppini, positioning the mushrooms and garlic around the meat. When just golden on both sides, remove the scaloppini and set aside.

Deglaze the pan with a splash of Marsala wine, then add the chicken stock, the balsamic vinegar and the remaining Marsala.

Reduce slightly, stirring constantly. It should be slightly sweet and earthy. Season to taste.

Add the scaloppini back into the pan and cook for another 30 seconds on each side.

Remove the scaloppini again and plate up onto warm plates.

Add the cream to the pan and stir well. As soon as it's combined, add the remaining butter and mix well but quickly.

Pour the sauce over the veal and garnish with chopped parsley.

Serve with: sautéed potatoes and sautéed spinach.

Drink: Chianti from a wicker-wrapped bottle.

OSSOBUCO

BONE WITH AN 'OLE

O SSOBUCO, Italian for 'bone with a hole', is a nineteenth-century Milanese dish of braised, cross-cut veal shanks (preferably cut from the top of the thigh for the best meat-to-bone ratio. Although traditionally served with Risotto alla Milanese, I prefer it with sautéed potatoes.

There are two types of Ossobuco: the original style, flavoured with gremolata, and a modern version that includes tomatoes. This one is inspired by my mother's recipe.

This dish is defined by the silken texture of the bone marrow. Eat it hot, scooped straight from the bone, on toast sprinkled with sea salt and parsley – hat-tip to Fergus Henderson.

YP

WHAT YOU NEED

Serves 4

Seasoned flour
4 x 3cm thick cuts of veal shank
100g pancetta
50ml olive oil
50g butter
250ml white wine
250ml chicken stock
1 carrot, finely chopped
A stick of celery, chopped
½ tsp each of salt and black pepper
1 tsp sugar
1 large onion, finely chopped
2 tins whole plum tomatoes
2 tbsp tomato puree
Thyme
1 bay leaf

FOR THE GREMOLATA
1 tbsp lemon zest
1 clove of garlic, minced
1½ tbsp flat leaf parsley, very finely chopped
1 tsp olive oil
A pinch of sea salt

WHAT YOU DO

Mix the carrot, onion, celery, bay leaf and thyme together with the veal shanks, then add the wine. Refrigerate for at least 2 hours to let the flavours develop – ideally overnight.

In a heavy-bottomed pan, gently heat the pancetta until it has rendered most of its fat. Remove and set aside. Add the butter and olive oil to the pancetta fat and heat. Separate the shanks from the marinade mixture and decant the wine. Fry off the carrots, celery and onion until golden brown. Add the tomato paste and fry for 30 seconds. Add the tinned tomatoes, breaking them up with a spoon. Add the chicken stock and the white wine, then the thyme and bay leaf from the marinade. Simmer gently over a low heat until the sauce is smooth.

Dredge the veal shanks in seasoned flour and fry off until golden brown. Add the browned veal shanks and pancetta to an ovenproof tray then add the sauce ensuring the shanks are completely covered. Cover tightly and cook at 180 °C for 2 hours (or preferably for several hours in a slow cooker).

Remove shanks, plate and pour over the sauce, having first removed the bay leaf and thyme stalks. Mix together all of the gremolata ingredients and sprinkle over the shanks before serving.

PARISERBØF

Hosted by DBC Pierre

Many coincidences flash through these chronicles; one is that Yianni and I first tasted this beef dish in the same bar in the same Jutland town at different times before meeting. Both of us stayed in Jutland after that, and ate it again and again. It still ranks as one of our top three big flavours, and neither of us can remember the end of the night we discovered we had it in common.

Then the job of unravelling history began.

The legendary provenance of this dish is simple: it was invented by a German bomb. More intriguing is how it grew from a mess blown through a battleship's galley into a Danish national delicacy. The dish's history, as strong and unique as its taste, is here written for the first time.

Two Courbet-class battleships, *Paris* and *Courbet* were called to Allied operational duty on 21 May 1940. The *Paris* was bombed barely three weeks later while defending the harbour at Le Havre; that blast destroyed a galley and blew up a food store before wrecking the hull.

But the *Paris* didn't sink. Officers pointed her towards Cherbourg and nursed her into port on a knife-edge; she was taking on 300 tons of water an hour. During that harrowing voyage it fell to someone to inspect below-decks before opening the galley to a tired and hungry crew. That officer is pictured at right; he quickly declared the galley beyond use.

The man on the left, thought to be D. T. Gorrent R.N., took a second look at the carnage of beef mince, egg, onion and twisted metal, all sprayed with fragments of vegetable pickle, a warship's staple – and saw a way forward. He saw that ingredients near the blast zone were seared, making a mix of cooked and raw food. Scraping beef and raw egg onto a tin plate, he added a handful of onion, beetroot, capers, and horseradish. Although it was a joke to bolster morale, those present when the plates came up declared it the finest meal they had ever eaten.

Everyone who tasted Paris Beef that day took the flavour with him; but only one must have made it again, as the dish is unknown in France.

How did it become celebrated Danish cuisine? Both Allied officers were only briefly attached to the French fleet. At the end of 1940, Gorrent transferred to a submarine base in Iceland, and in 1943 fathered a child there with a local girl; it was common during what Icelanders call 'The Situation', when troops outnumbered local men.

Mother and child were abandoned just as Iceland broke off from the Kingdom of Denmark in 1944. To avoid being foreigners on the mainland, the girl took her child to Jutland before the republic was declared. She worked at the *Rød Hest* tavern in Holstebro, where a menu card from 1945 shows that Paris Beef – *Pariserbøf* – had travelled with her.

Iceland became a republic that year, never suspecting its role in the spread of *Pariserbøf*; though anyone frequenting the clubs of Borgarnes, Iceland, may have heard the story in song – *Hvernig Segir Maður Pariserbøf-bøf-bøf* – by a young crooner of the day.

He is heir to this wartime photograph. The original recipe is scribbled on the back, and for that we dedicate this history to him: Torgren Torgrensson – the officer's abandoned child.

WHAT YOU NEED

Serves 1

170g fillet steak
Butter and vegetable oil for frying
Sea salt
Freshly ground black pepper
Brandy for flambéing
Thickly sliced white bread
1 very fresh egg yolk
Parsley, finely chopped

FOR THE ACCOMPANIMENTS
Tabasco sauce
Worcestershire sauce
1 tbsp capers
1 tbsp white onion, finely diced
1 tbsp roasted onions
1 tbsp pickled beetroot, finely diced
1 tbsp fresh horseradish, grated
1 tbsp sweet pickled cucumbers

WHAT YOU DO

Using a very sharp knife, cut the fillet steak into tiny pieces – just short of it being minced. Form the chopped meat into a patty, as evenly as possible, ideally in a round food mould.

Heat a teaspoon of vegetable oil in a heavy frying pan until it smokes. Add one teaspoon of butter and the meat patty. Season the top heavily with salt and pepper.

Cook for 45 seconds. Flip the meat and add another teaspoon of butter to the pan. Cook for a further 45 seconds. Flambé with the brandy.

Remove the meat from the pan and set aside. Pour off the juices and set aside.

Turn the heat down, add a tablespoon of butter to the pan and fry the bread on both sides until golden brown.

Remove the bread from the pan to the plate, put the meat on top and then pour the juices over both. Sprinkle with parsley and serve with the accompaniments on the side.

Pour the uncooked yolk onto the meat at the table and burst it so it seeps through the meat and into the bread.

Drink: Carlsberg Elephant beer and Underberg bitters.

MONTERREY BARBECUE

Courtesy of DBC Pierre

I F YOU make it as far as Monterrey from the Mexican border at Reynosa, then you've made it to Mexico. I say it because there's not one but two borders on the road – the Mexican border, and the second Mexican border, because the first one is so much of a good thing. If you get bitten at the first one you'll get bitten at the second; there's enough distance between them that they can call ahead. But when you're finally through, and the jagged peaks at Monterrey rise in the distance, this is the taste of that space between your last meal in Texas and the next one in Mexico.

WHAT YOU NEED

Serves 4–6

1.5–2kg of beef brisket with fat on
1 large red onion
1 fat jalapeño per serving
1 small can chipotle peppers

FOR THE RUB
2 tbsp sea salt
1 tbsp rough black pepper
2 tsp chilli powder
1 tsp garlic powder

FOR THE SAUCE
¼ cup of strong coffee
5 tbsp orange juice

3 tbsp balsamic vinegar
2 tbsp soy sauce
2 tbsp HP sauce
1 tbsp Worcestershire sauce
1 chipotle pepper

WHAT YOU DO

Heat an oven to 110 °C.

Slice the onion into 3 or 4 thick rounds and place in the bottom of an ovenproof pot to form a platform for the beef.

Mix up the rub and thoroughly coat the brisket before placing it on the onions fat-side up.

Mix the sauce, throw in the can of chipotle peppers, and pour around the onions.

Seal the pot, making it as airtight as possible; use a double layer of foil under the lid, for example. Weight it down if vapour escapes.

Then into the oven and cook for 5 hours.

Only check on the meat if you suspect moisture escapes from the pot.

Rest the beef in foil for 20 minutes after cooking, meanwhile pouring the juice, onions and chipotle into a blender to make a dipping gravy.

Thicken the gravy to taste by simmering in a pan while stirring in refried beans or 2 teaspoons of corn flour dissolved in cold water.

Fry the jalapeños until scalded, a couple of minutes each, and watch out for the vapour, it's pepper spray (recovering assailants might just want to eat the chillies raw).

Finally, slice the beef in the direction of the grain, let it fall into the lumps that it will, and serve on wax paper with a scalded jalapeño and pot of dipping juice on the side.

Goes well with homemade 'slaw and barbecue beans – just drain a can or two of barbecue beans, add a chipotle to the drained sauce, blend it and add back to the beans.

Monterrey Barbecue also makes a killer drowned sub; load some onto half a baguette and smother in gravy.

DIESEL & HONEY

A.K.A. EL DIESTRO

Courtesy of DBC Pierre

THE Diestro Diesel & Honey comes from a million-to-one-shot mixing gamble at a smoking bar in Mexico City. It is by a large margin the most weighty, mature, game-changing drink I have ever tasted. Discovered by libertine billionaires Antonio and Oscar, presumably after 999,999 lesser mixing accidents, it's a drink so well married to our aims that it could never have been invented deliberately. The principal ingredient, Agavero, has for over 150 years carried the ingredient damiana flower – shown to be a true aphrodisiac in clinical tests, and so effective as a herbal mood lifter that it's gradually being banned in states across the world. The final essence is of a whisky, but the kind we would have had if Scotland were in the Caribbean. Three of these can change your life.

WHAT YOU NEED

Agavero licor de tequila
Whisky, Johnnie Walker or Jameson's
Good ice

WHAT YOU DO

Fill a tumbler with hard ice. Pour 2 parts Agavero to 1 part whisky. Stir well.

Sit back and make love or make wishes.

```
***********************************

          DBC PIERRE

***********************************


1. BOOT HILL - STEVIE RAY VAUGHAN

2. PA LA PALOMA -
     ALQUIMIA LA SONORA DEL XXI

3. EL MONO - VERY BE CAREFUL

4. WHOLLE LOTTA ROSIE - THE KING

5. SAN FRANCISCO -
     ME FIRST AND THE GIMME GIMMES

6. SAGADORA HOT DUB (SHANTEL REMIX) -
     AMSTERDAM KLEZMER BAND

7. CUMBIA DEL SOL - CARMON RIVERO

8. COME AS YOU ARE - LITTLE ROY

9. PEOPLE EQUALS SHIT -
     RICHARD CHEESE

10. LA GRANGE - ZZ TOP

11. TOKYO SHOE SHINE BOY -
     PRINCESS AKATSUKI

12. JAMES BOND - ROLAND ALPHONSO

13. HELL HOUND ON MY TRAIL -
     ROBERT JOHNSON
```

FROM DUST

THE GOSPEL ON THE HILL

THE MEATliquor CHRONICLES
PART TWO

333 words (better half of the Beast)

INSIDE us lives a real being of meat and gods. When we meet someone new it asks only two questions: would we fuck them, or would we go over the hill with them. The hill is that hill between us and enemy fire, between us and unknown death. The meathill, in the meatspace, where Facebook fears to tread. Hill of the real. Hill endured by forefathers. Hill we must expect in order to live well; because when we expect it we're forced to ask the gods' question: who would we go over with. Would we go with Carol Vodafone. Would we go with Cilla Bang, the government, the market. Because these are the ones saying they will cover us at the hill.

But they won't cover us. Will they fuck.

If you are someone who would go to the hill, and you meet others who would go with you, then only you all should share your time and drink. To this nucleus add those you would fuck, sharing time and drink again – and so it is that societies are formed in our age.

But the hill is key. Go with a demon, go with a saint, if you're nobody go alone. But live a life prepared to go. Only this way are the right questions asked. If you would fuck and go over with the same person then it's godsent. But don't just fuck and drift away from us at the hill. A pact is a pact.

The lesson of this gospel is revealed at the most holy meatspace: Burning Man, where individuals gather to define the real, where the hill is mined for energy. Uncanny meetings can seem acts of chance, but in fact we identify fellow hillhounds at a distance, and unawares. Rejoice when this happens, for then we can say: yea though we walk through the valley of the shadow of death, we will fear no evil – for thou coverest me at the hill and thy drinks are fucking banging.

DBC

He meets a new friend but it is another demon.
Yea does the demon rejoice and follow him.
And so they are two

✝

A MEATing IN THE DUST

By Yianni Papoutsis

PART ONE

IT WAS the smell that woke me. It was pitch black in there, heightening my other senses. The noise was incredible: a brutal cacophony of explosions and bass tearing the night apart, rattling the plastic windows in their fibreglass frames. Primeval shrieks punctuated the maelstrom.

I'd passed out in an oven, awoken in a freezer. How long had I been out? An hour? A day? Longer? There was no frame of reference. I sat up, cracking my head on the ceiling a few inches above me.

Good morning.

Groping around blindly I felt duct tape beneath my fingers. Picking at it allowed me to peel away a corner of the tin foil covering the windows. Outside, a steel dragon belched flame at a crystal skull and went about its business.

I needed something to drink: coconut water. And coffee.

And whisky.

Also cigarettes.

And weed.

Rebalance the toxic chakras.

Whatever it took to drag myself from the safety of Morpheus' (or his sister Morphine's) tender embrace. I needed to leave that warm and friendly place and drag my sorry ass out into that mind-bending carnage out there … A world where acid-heads seek solace in the arms of their nightmare visions, knowing that no drug-fuelled hallucinations could ever be as sphincter-clenchingly, life-changingly disturbing as some of the things they see here in meatspace …

In The Dust. Fuck. What *was* that smell?

Fumbling with the head torch I wore wrapped around my wrist, a beam of light shot out though the darkness, catching a million Dust motes in its glare.

The Dust was everywhere.

On, and in everything and everyone.

The Dust *never* leaves you.

I clambered off the bunk, mashing my head into the ceiling again one more time for good measure and followed my nose to the source of the stench.

A small fridge clad in 1970s plastic wood sat there looking at me.

It said nothing.

This was worrying.

It should be purring away happily, content in its work of keeping our drinks cold.

Instead it was silent.

I checked around for the comforting glint of the LED.

I found the LED. Dark.

No gas.

I knelt down, opened the fridge, shut it again and puked into my mouth.

No beer.

Just chicken.

Chicken gone bad.

When things go bad in The Dust, they go bad quickly.

Having recovered enough to vent the smell of putrefying poultry, I set about repurposing the duct tape from the tin foil on the windows, sealing the fridge off and covering it with dire warnings scrawled in marker pen as to what vicious fate would befall anybody who opened it between now and the end of time.

The front door burst open. Clouds of Dust swirled in. A figure collapsed through the opening. The Dust coating him made it appear as if he were hewn from alabaster.

Or possibly ketamine.

I reached past the dishevelled figure and slammed the door shut.

'You cunt. What the fuck happened here? How did this place get so … so dusty … so fucking … destroyed? How long have I been out? And what the fuck happened to the sodding fridge? I woke up and it smelt like a fucking morgue in here.'

He looked up at me through Dust-encrusted goggles. Apart from those and a pair of Santa Claus boxer shorts, he was naked. Licking his cracked lips he stood up, trod on an empty whippet and fell straight back over again.

'Serves you right. Jesus H. Christ. We're fucked. I'm just glad the deposit for this juggernaut is on your card. The deposit is on your card isn't it? Oh fuck, I hope the deposit's on your card …'

He said nothing, merely pulled himself upright to sit at what had been our table. Sweeping a swathe of empty beer cans, whisky bottles, NOS canisters, Rizlas, cigarettes, Dixie Cups and limes onto the floor, he proceeded to skin up. His hands shook terribly. He was only barely in this world: his mind pulled a dozen different ways by a dozen different drugs, ravaged by dehydration and succumbing to the more advanced effects of sleep-deprivation; he was a husk of his former self. A twisted knot of psychoses held together by a cement of dust and psychedelics. This was a man on his way down. I, however, was on my way up.

Which way was up, though, wasn't yet clear.

I just knew I had to get out of there fast before I was sucked into his fug of a comedown.

It was then I remembered the beef. The freezer was full of minced chuck steak. The plan had been to make a massive chili for the camp but the only pots we had were tiny – barely big enough to boil an egg, let alone feed a hundred starving Burners.

I opened the freezer door, my mind reeling at what I might find. Miraculously the beef was still frozen solid. The freezer wasn't getting opened every two minutes like the fridge had been so it had stayed colder.

I got the beef out of the freezer to defrost and, grabbing my bug-out bag, goggles and gas-mask, I stepped out of the door and into The Dust.

PART TWO

Hours pass. For some, it may be days.

By this point the rigid fences we build around time have crumbled and become subjective: as some wax, others wane.

Night turns to day, cold turns to hot.

The fire of the flame-throwers gives way to the heat of the sun.

Giant mutant vehicles lumber through The Dust, each one carrying its brood of Burners on its back, like huge metal spiders.

Some are heading home for repairs, vehicles and occupants alike scarred and weary after the rigours of the night. Some hysterical, some silent, their minds desperately trying to process what they've seen. Others are just now heading out to Deep Playa by the Trash Fence to watch Robot Heart do battle with Disco Duck.

There are fewer explosions now.

There is still a lot of bass.

And hippies.

Fucking hippies everywhere …

PART THREE

Hours pass. For some, it may be days.

The Gods are angry today.

We have displeased the Elementals with our bacchanalian display the previous night.

The Sun is furious, unblinking and all-seeing, his blistering wrath slowly creeping into every shady refuge, leaving no place to hide.

Wind pulls Dust up into a twisting dance, angry whirlwinds writhing across the desert, unpredictable and devastating to whatever they touch.

Only Water is on our side.

Water is our only friend against the worst excesses of her brothers.

Water is sacred here.

Water makes ice for our whisky.

Masked figures appear through The Dust: road-weary travellers seeking the shelter of our camp.

Some have been awake for days. Others minutes.

All seem shell-shocked. All seek sustenance.

We have meat.

We have buns: Burners bring more.

We have pickles. Proper dill pickles.

Somebody has onions.

A girl with flashing lights in her hair brings ketchup and mustard.

A lettuce appears.

Then cheese slices.

We scavenge salt and pepper.

A small army of volunteers sets up a production line, shredding lettuce, chopping onions, saucing buns, slicing pickles. They cut themselves. A lot.

I fire up the gas stove and start heating a small cast-iron skillet. It is big enough for precisely one burger at a time.

We make burgers.

We feed Burners.

The MEATwagon is born.

MeatDaddy.

Black Rock City.

PLAYA SHAM-PAIN

Courtesy of Giles Looker

S OMEWHERE, out there in The Dust, there is a bar, as fleeting and ephemeral as its name. Its location changes according to the whim of The Placers.

A bar wherein many a Burn-weary soul has sought shelter from The Dust and The Heat.

Many have searched for it in vain.

Most have happened upon it by chance.

For some it is an airport lounge, for others a cruise-ship; still more remember it as a museum of curiosities or an island paradise, for it is many things to many people.

A sign, spray-painted hastily in two-foot letters on the back of the DJ booth, commands:

NO DUBSTEP

NO COLDPLAY

NO PSY-TRANCE

This is a bar for drinkers: 'No beer. Hard liquor only'.

Bring your own glass – there's none on offer at this bar. But there is ice and there are limes and there is liquor.

Search for it and it might find you.

YP

WHAT YOU NEED

Serves 1 Burner

Vodka – ideally Gordon's from a plastic jug
Block ice
Apple juice
Ginger ale
2 limes
A commando knife

WHAT YOU DO

Using the knife, hack a piece of ice from the block and place into whatever vessel the dusty traveller has brought with them.

Squeeze one and a half limes over the ice.*

Half-fill the vessel with vodka.

Top-up with apple juice and ginger ale.

Wipe the squeezed lime halves around the top of the vessel (helps prevent lips being destroyed by The Dust around the rim).

Garnish with remaining lime pieces.

Stir, using the commando knife.

Depending on their manners, before, during and after the afore-described process, proffer the icy beverage with a courteous bow or pour it on the floor.

* At the time of writing, the world is undergoing an apocalyptic lime shortage.

✝

THE BOOK OF LOOKER

As told to DBC Pierre
555 words (lovechild of the Beast)

INSTITUTIONALISED at birth and once rumoured to be a missing royal, Giles Looker's passage (through life) is a shadowy one, its trajectory hard to confirm. From his made-up name – an obvious anagram of *Goose Killer* – to the shocks of bright ginger hair, now known to be fastidiously dyed and straightened at an Eritrean salon in Bexleyheath, his CV has been largely pieced together from official documents and hearsay.

According to reports, after a promising start in ballroom dancing – one that earned him the nickname 'Turbofox' for his dazzling foxtrot – the young Looker increasingly grew withdrawn, associating with an ever smaller clique of young offenders at the home in Oxfordshire where he served his childhood. Carer notes from the time reveal that flagons of rhubarb brandy were once recovered from under his bed. The ensuing investigation showed a pattern spanning years, during which he had diligently squirrelled institutional puddings and even sugar from the tea table. Although nobody had ever fully believed he took eight sugars in his tea, the puddings showed particular insight and application, given that rhubarb was often alternated at random with prunes and tinned fruit.

Then a prune schnapps was discovered. A tropical punch quickly followed. From there the boy's path could only lead one way – and in the eyes of many it was down. His eventual departure from the home mysteriously coincided with a fire in the catering block, and while no direct accusations were ever made, one image stuck in the minds of many – a pair of specially sequinned dancing callipers laid beside a tree nearby.

What is known since about the 'Rain Man of cocktails' is that sometime after the Brink's-Mat robbery he was found pulling drinks at The Bull in Charlbury for Roy Flynn, once manager of the rock band Yes, and previous owner of sixties London's notorious speakeasy. Early CCTV footage later places him near the Hazardous Substances lab at Nottingham University, as well as at a local watering hole called Brass Monkey; authorities have since declared his university degree genuine, despite a diploma simply bearing the word 'substances' in an unsteady scrawl.

Sometime between Fred West's reign of terror and the death of the last Kray twin, Looker is known to have associated with cocktail legends Dick Bradsell, Dale DeGroff and Michael Butt at Match Bar in London, and by the time of Harold Shipman's last year in practice he had partnered with Butt in the notorious cocktail-laundering operation Soulshakers. Within a year even Scotland Yard was forced to admit he had achieved a position above law and was unstoppable. This was proved true when, after Dr David Kelly's tragic demise in a London park, evidence was submitted to authorities suggesting that Looker had been responsible for intoxicating as many as 30,000 people at a time, both at home and abroad, and was expanding his 'empire of ethanol' not only across award-winning clubs and bars, but intercontinental air routes as well. In a rare public statement traced to the landline at Chequers, Looker simply said: 'I have travelled the world making drinks and drinking drinks and can't believe I get paid to do something I really love.'

What is true is that this self-styled granddaddy of hipsters breaches cocktail bars around the world without regret, invited or not – and it seems increasingly not.

Investigations are ongoing.

BLOOD & DUST

A MELTING OF MINDS

Courtesy of Giles Looker

THIS is what I remember: it was the perfect morning; blue sky and not too hot. For some reason I noticed that there was no music coming from The Bar, a strange thing indeed. I ran in and it was empty. I headed back to the RV, grabbed my CDs, shouted at Smokey to pick himself up off the floor and come to The Bar. I poured myself an extra-large Margarita and played ska and reggae. Smokey came, fixed himself a drink and we played music. Then this little fella of Greek appearance strolls in … I fix him a drink and he fixes us a massive rail of something. It was the first time we met and this is where the party started.

Slowly but surely, more and more people joined the perfect day. We drank tequila, ice-cold beer; we danced; we chatted.

We played music and made drinks until the next day; it was our party and only just the beginning.

WHAT YOU NEED

50ml Arette Blanco
20ml lemon juice
20ml sugar syrup
45ml Californian red wine
3 dashes of absinthe (optional)

WHAT YOU DO

Place all ingredients into a cocktail shaker, shake over as much ice as you can get, then pour the contents into a glass and DRINK.

Smile.

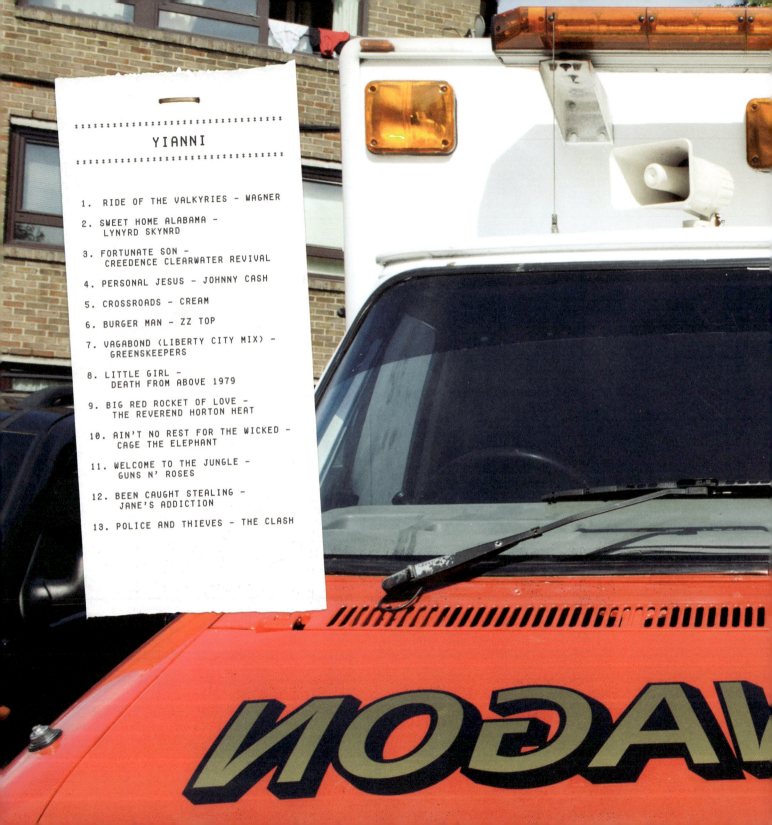

YIANNI

1. RIDE OF THE VALKYRIES - WAGNER

2. SWEET HOME ALABAMA -
   LYNYRD SKYNRD

3. FORTUNATE SON -
   CREEDENCE CLEARWATER REVIVAL

4. PERSONAL JESUS - JOHNNY CASH

5. CROSSROADS - CREAM

6. BURGER MAN - ZZ TOP

7. VAGABOND (LIBERTY CITY MIX) -
   GREENSKEEPERS

8. LITTLE GIRL -
   DEATH FROM ABOVE 1979

9. BIG RED ROCKET OF LOVE -
   THE REVEREND HORTON HEAT

10. AIN'T NO REST FOR THE WICKED -
    CAGE THE ELEPHANT

11. WELCOME TO THE JUNGLE -
    GUNS N' ROSES

12. BEEN CAUGHT STEALING -
    JANE'S ADDICTION

13. POLICE AND THIEVES - THE CLASH

THE GOSPEL OF THE WAGON

THE MEATliquor CHRONICLES
PART THREE

444 words (park and ride to the Beast)

A CHILD undirtied by lies is the first to see the glow and then the flames. They are as unambiguous to him as if the Virgin were arriving with a mambo band. He goes to them without knowing why. He feeds there and feels better but does not know why. All he knows as he stands torn between staying and going – is that a crowd comes from the horizon; and he knows not why.

But they say they do.

A nucleus of Quality has arrived out of nowhere. A truth. It appears like other nuclei and deals in the same materials but something is different, and that difference throbs as an impulse through crowds. All know but don't really know why they go. They just keep going.

What the child and the crowd see in the flames is a thing stripped bare, without parasites, without terms and conditions. A thing like every other thing of its kind, but isolated, fenced off and polished by itself, without traps or promises. What the child sees in the flames is not something to take away, but a space to be.

A sanctuary.

That nude thing glows hotter than any device designed throughout history. Its nakedness has been perfected, and is powerful because it calls us back to our roots. Those roots remind us: in the beginning there was flesh. We are made of it, and other creatures are made of it, and we eat each other for energy.

This is what we do.

The energy in flesh is far greater than the energy in grasses, and that excess power buys us time to stop foraging and think. We thought of flame. We started thinking about the hill, and painting it, and writing about it. We had time to cultivate. With satiety came leisure and with leisure ideas and with ideas progress and with progress intoxicants like killer rye whiskey.

These things, together the root and the result of all meatkind, are what the child saw in the flames. They existed everywhere – but their spirit and truth appeared only here, distilled. And he wanted to stay. That spirit infected all hillhounds who gathered, and there, cradled between the origins of intelligence and the tools we designed to dull it back down, they were themselves, and they felt all right. They saw that the Nativity had no grasses, except to feed cow and lamb.

It was a gospel that must be spread; one that spoke for itself through flames and smoke. And lo, The Wagon brought it to the people, and they came. Not a bandwagon that would decline, mined and undermined and sold as promises.

But a MEATwagon.

DBC

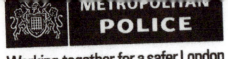

METROPOLITAN POLICE

Working together for a safer London

Crime Reference number: ████████████
Date: 7 December, 2010

Mr Ioannis Papoutsis
████████████████████████
████████████████████

Metropolitan Police Service

████████████████████████
████████████████████████
████████████████████████
████████████████████

Telephone: ████████████████
Facsimile: ████████████████
e-mail:

www.met.police.uk

Dear Mr Papoutsis

We are very sorry that you have become a victim of a crime. Thank you for reporting this matter to us.

We have reviewed the crime but so far there is not enough evidence to continue with further inquiries and the case will now be closed. However, if we get any new evidence we will of course act on that new information.

We appreciate that this decision may be disappointing to you – unfortunately, not all crimes reported to us lead to an arrest. However, by reporting crimes you can help us police your local area more effectively. The Safer Neighbourhoods Team and their police community support officers (PCSOs) work with your local community to tackle local issues and problems. You can find details of your local team at www.met.police.uk/saferneighbourhoods.

Further information

- We have enclosed a leaflet, 'Victims of Crime – support and advice', with this letter. It gives you more information on the Criminal Justice Service, contact details for support organisations in London and details of how you may be able to claim compensation through the Criminal Injuries Compensation Authority (CICA).

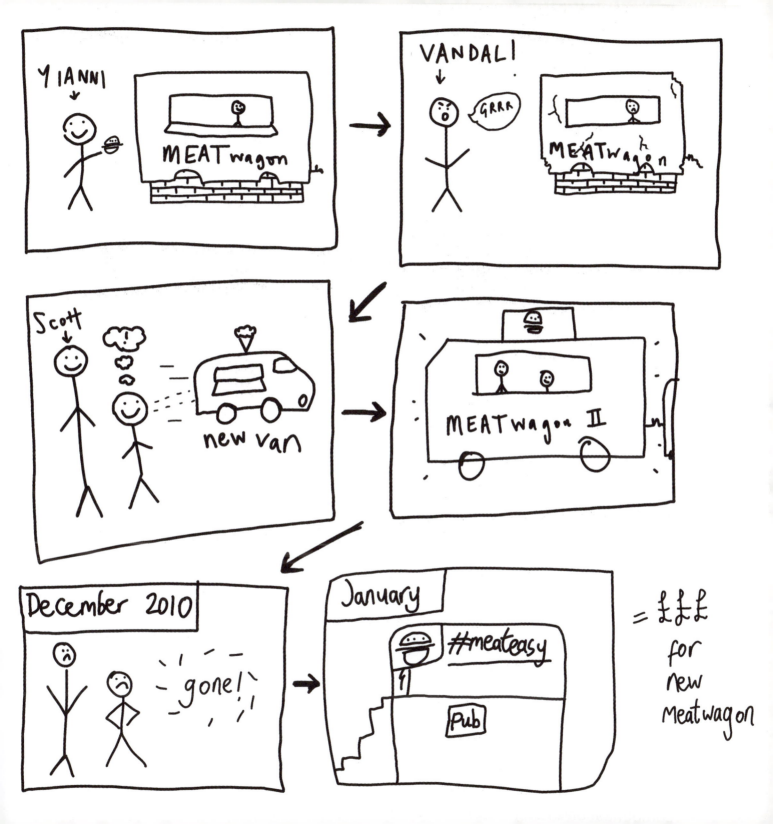

✝

SCOTT COLLINS

333 words (shadow of the Beast)
As told to DBC Pierre

BORN one of a pair of boys into a sunny Kent milieu, Scott Collins is said to have never lived through a winter, due to the permanent aura of golden light which could be seen emanating from his trouser. So compelling was the phenomenon that he became a muse for local nobility, who would queue to paint him in a variety of settings, in his now-famous sailor's suit. Among nobles to clamour for his image was Lord Henry Wotton – Hank, to his friends, and to the young Scott. It was this opinionated libertine who, having painted the infant muse in every setting and position, suggested the child should have his brother painted instead, while he went off to taste all the pleasures life had to offer.

So it was that young Collins charted a course for sensation. It soon became clear that with each forbidden fruit, each drink or substance, paintings of his brother aged grotesquely, while Collins retained his boyish charm. His allure was soon in demand in venues the world over, where a whole generation of sensualists believed they too could survive the depravity and excess of their golden host. From Los Angeles to London to Val d'Isere no rake was left uninfluenced by Collins, who quickly set about opening his own boutique venues in order to concentrate his growing powers. Fatefully one day, happening upon an ordinary pub, he decided that these, too, should lose their vulgar, workmanlike natures, and no less than thirteen pubs were opened thereafter, all bearing Collins's hallmark of painless decadence. To this day he retains eight of them, including The Clarence of Balham, said to be where a young Norwegian royal was divinely impregnated, which story led to the pub being voted London's pub of the year by the *Evening*

Standard. Since then a host of scantily clad aristocrats have been spotted loitering in the venues, while paintings of his brother, to have been auctioned at Sotheby's later this year, have reportedly turned to dust.

SCOTT'S MUM'S SCHOOL SANDWICHES

M Y MOTHER has many, many talents. Cooking was never one of them (although vastly improved now). Having three sons and a job she was always time-starved so came up with a cunning way of bulk-preparing sandwiches for the lunchboxes.

Should make one serving per child (three in this case) for each school day for a month.

This is why I taught myself to cook, chose Home Economics as a subject (the only boy in a class of 30 to do so), and became infatuated with food.

Thanks, Mum xxxxxx

Scott

WHAT YOU NEED

6 loaves Mother's Pride white sliced bread
2l tub margarine
A mountain of pre-sliced ham (the more lurid pink the better)
*   with extra jelly around the edges if the budget stretches*
A catering pack of cling film/glad wrap
Palette knife
Bread knife

WHAT YOU DO

Spread as many slices of bread out to cover a clean work surface, keeping the slices uniform and crust to crust (no gaps).

Using palette knife spread all slices liberally with margarine.

Carefully (as fast as you can) lay a square slice of ham on every other slice of bread.

Place one ham-less slice onto a hammed one.

Stack 4 or 5 of these on top of each other and slice in half. Diagonally or horizontally (it really doesn't make a blind bit of difference to the taste).

Pass the mound to one of your 'little helpers' who will then enthusiastically wrap them individually in cling film.

Toss all finished lunchtime 'treats' into the freezer.

Remove 3 frozen articles on morning of school and pack into lunchboxes.

Fingers crossed they will have defrosted by lunchtime.

Drink: Kia-Ora.

CHOC STAR
BROWNIE FUDGE SUNDAE

Courtesy of Petra Barran

I FIRST heard about Yianni and his MEATwagon in the summer of 2009 and knew that with his burgers and my brownies we should get together and make sweet music. We'd pull up outside pubs and parties, canals and shopping centres, and the gear that we were selling would be mutually supporting. All the burger fans would traipse halfway across London to get their chops round some of Yianni's meat and I'd be there in the choc-mobile to provide the pudding. Mainly they were one-track minded on the burger front, but I'd often see a shimmer of excitement for non-burger-related flavour sensations as they eyed some of the wares on my counter.

The Brownie Fudge Sundae was my bestseller from Choc Star, the van that I ran from 2005 to 2011. I'd serve it to all kinds of people – emos in Esher and grannies in Barnes, skaters in Bristol and diabetics in Glasgow. They all went wild for it, such is the great combination of the fudgy brownie, dense, vanilla-specked ice cream and molten dark, dark chocolate sauce that I'd squeeze over it so that it cascaded down those ice cream and brownie contours like hypnosis. Everyone would go super-quiet as they'd watch this sundae being brought to life – this, I can tell you, is one of life's truths: silence when watching hot choc sauce flowing.

When Yianni set up #MEATEASY it was those brownies he called in again to act as dessert, and though both it and Choc Star are now resigned to the vaults, that combo of burgers and brownies has formed the basis of my friendship

with Yianni, as we've both branched off into other areas of itinerant, free-wheeling food in London.

We go by the fudge-factor school of thought for brownies: a nice, glossy, almost meringue-like top, breaking easily into the deeply dense cake and with a good swathe of satisfying fudginess at the centre.

WHAT YOU NEED

Get hold of a proper, non-stick baking pan – the size of a roasting pan is perfect.

For the ice cream, I recommend getting hold of the best you can find. I would source mine from a great supplier in Herefordshire, but there's nothing wrong with a bit of Häagen-Dazs from the supermarket.

For the chocolate, I use a 70% Fairtrade organic blend – it's nice and fruity. In the supermarket I would recommend Valrhona Guanaja if you're near a Waitrose, or else Lindt 70% or Green & Black's 72%.

Makes 24

375g 70% chocolate
250g butter (salted)
1 tbsp cocoa powder
2 tsp espresso powder
6 large eggs (free range)
670g caster sugar
115g self-raising flour
150g walnuts – in pieces

FOR THE CHOCOLATE SAUCE
2 parts double cream
1 part muscovado sugar
1 part 70% chocolate, chopped
A splash of espresso or a pinch of granules

Vanilla ice cream

WHAT YOU DO

For the Chocolate Sauce: put cream and sugar in a saucepan on a low to medium heat and bring to the boil, stirring gently, so the sauce looks like caramel. Remove from heat and stir in chopped dark chocolate. Whisk until blended, add a splash or sprinkle of espresso to give it some edge, and then a drop of milk if it is too thick for your tastes. You can't really go wrong with this, however you decide to make it.

Pre-heat oven to 165 °C on fan/180 °C non-fan.

Line pan with baking parchment.

Put the walnuts in the pan and toast for 10 minutes – take out and leave on side in pan to cool.

Melt the chocolate with the butter in a Bain Marie. When a good way to being melted add the espresso powder and cocoa powder and stir until smooth.

Meanwhile, mix the sugar with the eggs. Give it a nice beating – preferably by hand.

Add the melted choc mixture and give another good stir. Sift in the flour.

Add the toasted walnuts and mix together.

Pour mix into the pan and bake until done – not too firm, not too liquid – around 45 mins.

Cool on trays.

Top each brownie with a good dollop of ice cream and smother in chocolate sauce.

Amazing eaten warm – but, interestingly, brownies can taste better, more intense a day or so after baking. Give it a go.

MEATloaf

BAD ATTITUDE

Hosted by DBC Pierre

MEATLOAF the singer preceded the dish he's named after, at least in this case; but for anyone who played their best air guitar to 'Bat out of Hell', this recipe is our shot at heaven by a stovetop light. While you warm the oven, ponder these little-known facts about the dish's namesake:

★ Bat out of Hell, *according to the* Guinness Book of Records *was the highest-selling UK album of all time, spending 470 weeks in the charts, and the third-highest globally with more than 30,000,000 copies sold.*

★ *Meatloaf went on a branded diet replacement plan in the early '90s and lost 84 pounds. It netted him $1,000,000.*

★ *Meatloaf doesn't actually like meatloaf.*

★ *Meatloaf was offered the lead in* Phantom of the Opera *but turned it down. Thank fuck.*

★ *Meatloaf fell off stage and broke his leg at a Toronto concert in 1978, finishing the tour in a wheelchair.*

★ *Meatloaf has been concussed 17 times.*

★ *Meatloaf is diabetic.*

★ *Meatloaf didn't eat meat for 15 years before deciding to give it a try. Pork chops floated his boat more than anything.*

Bat out of Hell was Yianni's first music purchase. I already had it, and was doing the dashboard-light thing by then; but it's never too late for air guitars to meet. Put on the disc and gather these ingredients for the loaf.

WHAT YOU NEED

1 red pepper
3 cloves
1 onion
2 cloves of garlic
1 carrot
1 stick of celery
A healthy splash of olive oil for frying
A small knob of butter for greasing
1kg minced chuck steak
1 cup bread crumbs
2 eggs
A good dose of Worcestershire sauce
2 pinches salt
A generous sprinkling of freshly ground black pepper
A pinch of cayenne pepper
A pinch of chilli powder
A couple of pinches of mixed dried herbs (Italian mix works well)

FOR THE GLAZE
2 tbsp ketchup
2 tbsp Dijon mustard
2 tbsp brown sugar

WHAT YOU DO

Preheat your oven to 180 °C.

Finely chop the garlic, onion, carrot, celery and red pepper. Sweat the vegetables in a frying pan over a low heat in the olive oil and butter until the onions are translucent, being careful not to burn the garlic. (You can always add the garlic halfway through if you don't trust yourself.)

When cool enough to handle, add the vegetable mixture to the minced chuck steak together with the rest of the ingredients. Mix well with your hands.

At this point you can put the mixture into a greased loaf tin or form it into a loaf shape on a greased baking tray depending on what you've got to hand and how you want it to look. Wet your hands slightly to stop the mix sticking to them.

Stick it in the oven for about half an hour. Meanwhile get the glaze ready: simply mix the sugar, ketchup and mustard together in a bowl.

Remove the loaf and spread the glaze over the top. Put it back into the oven for another half-hour or so. If you've got a probe thermometer, the centre should reach 70 °C.

Remove when it's done and let it cool for half an hour. If you try and cut it before it's had a chance to rest it'll just fall to bits.

Cut into slices and serve with mashed potatoes and …

Alternatively it's great, hot or cold, in sandwiches, ideally toasted with some Swiss cheese, mustard and gherkins (which is how we serve it at the MEATwagon).

LAYOVER CHILI

MEAT AND SPICE AND ALL THINGS NICE

CHILI is the archetypal American comfort food. Spend any time in the States and you'll see it everywhere, from diners to fast-food outlets to high-end restaurants.

They take it seriously too: Chili cook-offs take place all over the States and they're no laughing matter – some of them attract tens of thousands of people, and tempers have been known to fray under the influence of too much sun, too much beer and way too many Scoville units …

Every family, state, town and restaurant has its own take on this dish and I've encountered a seemingly infinite number of variations on the basic Chili recipe.

I call this Layover Chili as it's made specifically to be served over other things; hence, the idea is to end up with a smooth 'sauce' rather than a lumpy stew: it's a bastardisation of a Brown Chili 'sauce' popular in Washington DC where they serve it over burgers, spaghetti, fries – anything.

This is by no means an Ultimate Chili recipe – it's more of a basic structure on which you can build your own personal Chili. Have some fun with it.

If you like your Chili 'red', replace some of the beef stock with chopped canned tomatoes or a jar of passata. Like it smoky? Stick some chipotles in there.

In my opinion, Chili should never have beans in it – if you absolutely must have them, cook them separately (in pork fat) and serve them on the side.

With the spices, the trick is to add them over a long period of time, bit by bit, tasting as you go, until you hit that sweet spot.

Personally, I like to up the amount of cumin, oregano and chilli.

At MEATliquor this is laid over the top of our Chili Fries and Chili Dogs. There's always a huge cauldron of the stuff simmering away in the corner and you'll often find hungry chefs hurriedly slurping bowls of it out back as a quick pick-me-up before a busy service.

YP

WHAT YOU NEED

Serves 4–8 (depending on what you have with it and how greedy you are)

1.5l beef stock
1kg minced chuck steak
2 finely diced white onions
3–4 large cloves of garlic, minced
1 tbsp tomato paste
A significant amount of ground cumin
A large pinch each of chilli powder, cayenne pepper, paprika and black pepper
A hefty sprinkle of ground coriander
A good shake of dried oregano
A handful of minced pickled jalapeños
A squirt of ketchup
A similarly sized squirt of French's mustard
A bottle of beer
Salt and pepper

FOR THE GARNISH
Grated cheese
Minced onions
Mustard
Minced jalapeños

WHAT YOU DO

Gently sauté the onions and garlic in a large pot. Remove and set aside just as they start to brown.

Fry the beef and the tomato paste until it's a deep brown. Break it up as fine as it will go. Add the beef stock and deglaze the pan with the beer. The liquid should completely cover the meat. If it doesn't, add some beer.

Add the sautéed onions and garlic. Add the minced jalapeños and the spices. Don't add any salt – there's already loads in the stock.

Adjust the spicing to your taste, adding little bits at a time and letting it cook in for 5 minutes before tasting. Don't be shy with the spicing: it's a Chili, not a Bolognese. You should be able to taste the earthy flavour of the cumin through the hot stuff … Adjust the balance with a couple of squirts of ketchup and mustard.

Keep it simmering over a low heat for at least a couple of hours: the longer the better. Stir it occasionally.

Now's the time to adjust the seasoning with a bit of salt and pepper. Once again – go easy on the salt.

If more liquid is needed, add more beer.

Ideally, let it rest after cooking for at least an hour. It actually gets significantly better if you leave it overnight and eat it the following day.

Serve over nachos, hot dogs, spaghetti, burgers, fries … whatever, really. Top with mustard, grated cheese, minced jalapeños and some minced white onions.

Just make sure there's lots of ice-cold beer on hand …

THE DEAD ELVIS

Hosted by Pedro 'El Malo'

THE KING died 'taking care of business'. But we can't go into that – know why? Not because we didn't have perhaps the world's most intimate relationship with the King himself – ask any cunt who was at our childhood birthday parties – but because for some fucking reason, unlike the deaths of Buddy Holly, Roy Orbison and Johnny Cash, our man Elvis attracted something like the population of Argentina's worth of really fucked-up impersonators, who now dispute every fucking thing as if it had been them.

So get this: if you're that little cunt who not only doesn't look like Elvis but has to buy enough hair for sideburns and can't sing worth a shit – YOU ARE NOT THE FUCKING KING. If you're that sixty-year-old cunt who's fatter than four Elvises taped together and can't sing worth a shit – YOU ARE NOT THE FUCKING KING. Get it? If you're that cunt from the other week, who looks more like a fucking girl on hormones, and can't sing worth a fucking shit – TU NO ERES EL FUCKING KING. COMPRENDE?

Jesus Christ.

All of you are not only not the King but he would have fucking shat himself laughing and told you all to fuck off. Because here's the truth:

WE are the King.

We died taking a dump. Big deal, it fucking happens, get the fuck over it.

THIS – is our favourite recipe.

And we have fucking left the building.

WHAT YOU NEED

Peanut butter (crunchy or smooth – it's your choice)
Jam (the cheap, jelly-like stuff works really well here)
White bread (you want something like Mother's Pride or Kingsmill, preferably medium sliced)
Cooked crispy bacon
1 banana, sliced lengthways
7 Up or similar (full fat, NOT diet)
Plain flour
Oil for deep frying
Icing sugar for dusting

WHAT YOU DO

Preheat the oil to 170 °C.

Spread peanut butter on one slice of bread. Spread jam on the other slice of bread. Add bacon and banana. Bring together the two slices to form a sandwich. (Do I really need to explain this?) Stick the sandwich in the freezer for a little while to firm it up. Mix the flour and 7 Up into a smooth batter. It should be a bit thicker than pancake batter.

Remove the sandwich from the freezer and cut into 4 triangles. Dip each triangle in the batter and put them straight into the hot oil. Cook in batches according to the size of your pan/fryer. Overcrowd them and they'll stick together. Deep fry until golden brown. Remove from oil and drain on kitchen towel. Let them cool down for a few minutes before you tuck in: the filling's like peanut-flavoured magma when you first get them out of the fryer.

Dust with icing sugar and serve with vanilla ice cream. Or forget all that and just eat them straight from the kitchen counter.

Drink: with shame.

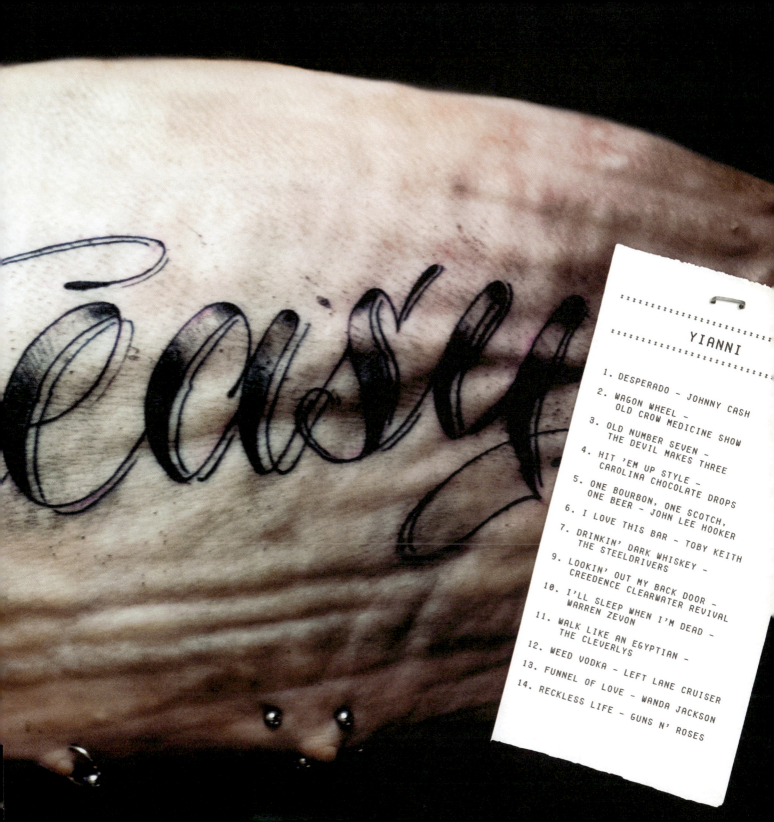

YIANNI

1. DESPERADO - JOHNNY CASH
2. WAGON WHEEL - OLD CROW MEDICINE SHOW
3. OLD NUMBER SEVEN - THE DEVIL MAKES THREE
4. HIT 'EM UP STYLE - CAROLINA CHOCOLATE DROPS
5. ONE BOURBON, ONE SCOTCH, ONE BEER - JOHN LEE HOOKER
6. I LOVE THIS BAR - TOBY KEITH
7. DRINKIN' DARK WHISKEY - THE STEELDRIVERS
9. LOOKIN' OUT MY BACK DOOR - CREEDENCE CLEARWATER REVIVAL
10. I'LL SLEEP WHEN I'M DEAD - WARREN ZEVON
11. WALK LIKE AN EGYPTIAN - THE CLEVERLYS
12. WEED VODKA - LEFT LANE CRUISER
13. FUNNEL OF LOVE - WANDA JACKSON
14. RECKLESS LIFE - GUNS N' ROSES

ON THE SAFETY OF NUMBERS

THE MEATliquor CHRONICLES
PART FOUR

333 words (halfway home)

ENEMIES hide in crowds. It's predictable. Among us walk the pointless, not of this world but from a level of tireless hell, a place where braying and lowing chime off bleaching bones, where sounds are thin, double-seared to release their fat, where no mysteries play because all is clear and open, this hell. This is where the pointless roam, munching without pleasure for lifetimes, their ignorant flesh all sagging and thick, without a trace of the patina that fooled us at first. Here they live in a stench of sweet ordure, hearing whistles and moos like whirring clocks, without passion or fat, waxy chins glistening dumbly under pointless words.

Before the third bone of chicken is clean, He said, one of you will betray me. And the wagon was razed, and when a new wagon came, it was stolen. Forces massed against the MEATdaddy, and like Napoleon he had to ask what forces he could amass against such hard cases; and the answer was – harder cases still. Of their ilk but also of this world, not demons but controllers of demons.

And to marshal demons one has to own the places they inhabit.

Lo, there came a man bearing on his skin the marks of legion; and he did own the places where demons supped and played. I will lend you a place, he said, to do with as you must. One Hellhound was placed on a lead at the door, to filter the worthy from the unworthy, who in any case were very few. MEAT was adored again, and the faithful came in ever greater number, up the road, round the back, up the stairs and past the Hellhound. The MEATdaddy, the

drinkmaker and the marshal of legions were three.

And did the MEATdaddy look around himself early one morning, through the bacchanal, past the Hellhound into the sky – and ask himself if he had in fact made a pact with a devil.

The answer burned him – yes, it said.

Thank fuck.

DBC

'My name is Legion,' he replied,
'for we are many'

✝

HIGH ENERGY

WORKING A KITCHEN SHIFT
AT #MEATEASY

By Helen Graves, Kitchen Gimp

KITCHEN Gimp. Or, me on a Wednesday night in the #MEATEASY kitchen. What was I thinking? I had actually, genuinely volunteered myself to spend an evening at the bottom of the kitchen food chain. I would report to the Grill Boss flipping the burgers, the Fry Bitch in charge of, um, frying stuff, the Burger Bed Prepper ... I would report to every man, and every man's dog. I was, in short, their bitch.

So what does General Gimping involve? Well, there's the cutting of burger buns for a start. It's an important job, you know, cutting those buns evenly. Slicing into your hand is optional, and to be honest I wouldn't really recommend it. Onion ring splitting is obviously up there with the important shit too – actually quite difficult and generally regarded in the kitchen as 'the most annoying job in the world'. Any membrane must be carefully removed because if it gets into the batter it's a nightmare to get out and it increases the danger of the onion slipping out of the ring, sticking to your chin and burning it. Now that's the most annoying thing in the world.

Other duties included weighing out beef. A whole lot of beef. The smell! The smell of the fresh meat was boss. I weighed it, rolled it into balls and stored 'em just how the Grill Boss liked 'em, ready for him to flatten on the grill. I washed up. I fished manky, unidentifiable crud out of plugholes. I basically rotated my way around various Gimp tasks, pausing only to take a swig from my ever-present Meantime beer, drink a shot, or eat a wayward chicken wing deemed not crisp enough to leave the kitchen. Every now

and then my razor-sharp focus would be interrupted by a call for 'MORE FORKS, GIMP!' 'cause #MEATEASY really didn't have enough forks.

Working in that place was exhilarating though: the energy was so high you'd have had to be dead inside not to get caught up in it. It sounded like it was going off on the other side of the pass; I couldn't see the customers but I sure could hear them. The bell rings to mark another order up; a glass breaks; a cheer; someone turns the music up. I think I even volunteered myself a second time for on-demand Gimping because it was so much fun. I set a trend; everyone wanted to get into that kitchen. Since when has glorified KP been a desirable job? Perhaps they wanted to spy and steal the secrets behind the best burgers in London? Well, I know some and I ain't telling.

The atmosphere in the #MEATEASY was unique and electric; an energy that could come only from a bunch of people who were doing something from the heart. In a rare moment of Gimp rest I pause to look at Yianni and think back to the time I first got my gob around a MEATwagon burger. It's been a rocky road but I marvel at how far he's come, and as I sink my teeth into a fresh Dead Hippie I wish him all the success in the world.

PECKHAM CURRY GOAT DIP SANDWICH WITH COCONUT COLESLAW

Courtesy of Helen Graves

NOBODY wanted to know about Peckham when I first lived here. Nobody wanted to know when I started writing about it either; about the food, the people. Especially not the people. Six years ago, Peckham still meant Del Boy and Damilola Taylor. It meant council blocks and gang crime, police tape and headlines. At least, it did to 'outsiders'. Now, the area is supposedly 'trendy'. We are, apparently, the 'new Dalston'. Vomit.

Five years ago I stumbled across a man in a van, in a car park, in an industrial estate in Peckham. His sign very neatly displayed the words 'Meat Wagon' and by 'neatly' I mean hand-scrawled in 'man writing', all self-conscious finger spaces and curly-tailed Ys. He was flipping burgers and telling tales of adventures in America; we chatted for ages about the benefits of frying chillies in butter and the best ratio of fat to meat in a burger. I marvelled at his use of a sourdough bun and his method of steaming the finished burger under a cloche. When I look back now to that half-hour space in time, it seems like it was almost the start of something, like one minute it was just me and Yianni standing in the middle of a car park in Peckham being geeky about food and then BOOM! Suddenly the people were coming.

That was before the money arrived in Peckham, before we had a greengrocer selling Neal's Yard cheese and salted capers, before the butcher selling aged rib eye and grouse, before the annual 'pop-up' Campari bar on top of a disused car park. I don't resent these additions to Peckham; hell, I enjoy them as much as the next white, middle-class young professional, but for me, the 'old Peckham' is still where it's at. This is where I can shop for plantains, yams and scotch bonnet chillies, thanks to the African communities who settled here. This is where I can buy a bowl of four bulbous aubergines for a pound. Herbs come in bunches you could use to sweep a chimney. Shopping in Peckham is an assault on the senses, as anyone who has walked through it on a hot summer's day will testify. The smell of old fish and scrawny broiler chickens is not easy to forget. Neither is the feeling of a flip-flopped foot plunged into the drainage streams of defrosting tropical fish. There's the ever-present whine of metal sawing through bone. The sounds of Arabic pop meet gospel meet dancehall.

There's a man who sells me goat meat. We have the same conversation every time. 'Making curry goat?' He smiles. I smile. He knows the answer. 'I can't believe you eat those hot peppers! Very hot!' He laughs at the little white girl with her taste for the flavours of Africa and the Caribbean. Peckham has inspired me as a cook more than any other place I have lived or visited. Here I learned about brown stew chicken, salt fish and jerk. You think white girls can't jerk? Think again. My own recipe marinade flies off the shelves in local shops. You think white girls can't curry goat? I think you know what's coming.

This is a kick-ass recipe both in the sense that it tastes really fine but also because the heat of the scotch bonnet chillies will lift you to a higher state of consciousness. You could tone it down, I suppose, but then you should also consider not being such a fucking pussy.

WHAT YOU NEED

FOR THE CURRY POWDER (MAKES A SMALL JAR)
15g coriander seeds
Seeds from 7 cardamom pods
15g black peppercorns
10g fenugreek seeds
5g ground turmeric
15g ground ginger
10g ground cinnamon

FOR THE CURRY
1kg goat meat, diced (or use mutton)
2 onions, finely chopped
3 spring onions, roughly chopped
2 cloves garlic, crushed
1 scotch bonnet chilli, slit down the middle but left whole
  (or use two if you like it really hot)
2 tomatoes, diced
2 tbsp finely chopped coriander plus extra to garnish
Small sprig thyme, leaves only
1 tsp cumin seeds
1 tsp curry powder for marinating, 1.5 tbsp for cooking
1 bay leaf
1 tbsp caster sugar
500ml lamb stock (or use water)
2 tbsp vegetable or groundnut oil, for frying

FOR THE COCONUT COLESLAW
¼ red cabbage, core removed and very finely sliced
1 large carrot, grated coarsely or cut into very fine strips
2 spring onions, very finely sliced
6 tbsp coconut milk
Juice of 1 lime
Small bunch coriander leaves, chopped
Salt and pepper

WHAT YOU DO

Grind the whole spices in a spice grinder or pestle and mortar and mix well with the ready-ground spices. Store in an airtight jam jar or container.

Mix the goat meat with 1 tsp of the curry powder, the spring onions, coriander and thyme. Mix well and refrigerate overnight or for at least 6 hours.

Heat the oil in a large, heavy based pan. Dust the marinade off the goat meat, reserving the marinade in the bowl. Brown the meat in batches. Set aside. Add a little more oil to the pan if necessary, then fry the onions gently for 20–30 minutes, until softened and starting to caramelise. Add the 1.5 tbsp curry powder, cumin, tomatoes, scotch bonnet, bay leaf and garlic. Cook for a few minutes, stirring, then add back the meat.

Add the stock plus 500ml water (or use 1 litre water instead) to the bowl that contained the marinade, rinsing it around to pick up all the residue, then add this to the pan with the sugar and the goat. Bring to the boil, turn down the heat, cover and simmer for approximately 2 hours, or until the meat is very tender. Uncover and simmer for a further hour to thicken the gravy. Check the seasoning and serve.

To make the coconut coleslaw, mix the vegetables together in a large bowl. Add the lime juice and coconut milk and some salt and pepper. Mix well and stir in the coriander.

To assemble the sandwich, pile some chunks of goat meat and coleslaw onto a lightly toasted white bun. Serve a pot of the curry goat sauce on the side for dipping.

'SLAW

T HERE'S variations on coleslaw to be found all around the world. Some are heavy on the mayo, some favour pickles. This is the one we serve at MEATliquor and is based on a Southern mustard slaw. Salting the cabbage first will draw out excess water and keep it extra crunchy.

YP

WHAT YOU NEED

Serves 8 as a side

2 white cabbages
1 red cabbage
4 large carrots
2 large white onions
Bunch curly parsley
1 tsp salt and ½ tsp finely cracked black pepper
250ml mayonnaise
2 tbsp wholegrain mustard
20ml white wine vinegar

WHAT YOU DO

Finely chop cabbage, carrots and onions. Sprinkle salt and pepper on the raw vegetables, mix well and wait for 30 mins. Remove any excess liquid from the veggies. Add remaining ingredients and mix through. Leave to sit for at least an hour. Adjust vinegar, salt, pepper and mustard to taste before serving.

Eat it with: anything greasy. Ideally fried chicken.

✝

A LOVE POEM*

By Jozef Alexis Marlow

The anticipation of our meeting makes my tummy
go all funny.

I make sure I dress appropriately – hair tied back;
Never wear white, always wear black.

I go to the cashpoint and draw out twenty,
Not sure what it will cost. I hope it's plenty.

The grin on my face tells you that I am near,
For now it is our time, my love, my dear.

I arrive and get seated, but I can't sit still
Another beer please, I just need to chill.

I wait for my number, I listen real close,
Fifty-six is called. 'That's me,' I boast.

I go to the counter and state my demands,
Then a waiting game, with sweaty palms.

Oh Meat East, #MEATEASY how I love thee;
A tear I will shed once you have left me.

It could be twenty minutes, an hour, or three,
But not long now, until you meet me.

I sip my beer, glance up at my friend.
He tells me a story, about life and its end.

Jozef, Jozef, I hear my name called.
I scream 'I'm here,' ever so bold.

This is the moment I have been waiting for.
This is the MEATing of LOVE COOKED RAW.

As I bite into you my mouth collapses.
Run free, my taste buds, you are no longer captive.

Oh #MEATEASY, how I love you so;
A tear I will shed when you have to go.

Oh Meat East, #MEATEASY how I love thee;
A tear I will shed once you have left me.

fin

* This poem is one of the more refined libations
offered to #MEATEASY during its time.

61

MAC 'N' CHEESE

Hosted by Torgren Torgrensson

IMAGINE my surprise when I entered a room I thought to be a hamburger establishment, and found myself facing a paramilitary chain gang in full cry. Such was the brutality and size of its agitators – above 100 kilograms and armed with knives and hammers – that I was greatly discomforted, and was forced to sit down. Among the swarthy brutes, who barked a ruthless tongue unknown beyond that door, I also spied a number of beautiful women. I touched one and she flew back at me, causing three broken ribs and a change of trousers before dinner. Mysteriously, all knew by instinct alone that my pet name was 'Knut', in the old Icelandic pronunciation. 'Out of the kitchen, Kunt!' they barked, and I sang along, increasingly happy with my choice of venue for dinner. Here follow the notes I took of their brutal anthem, punctuated with thorough beatings and cries:

Serves 6

500g dry macaroni
65g butter (plus 3 tbsp for sweating onion and garlic)
65g plain flour
500ml whole milk at room temperature
½ small onion, finely diced
1 clove garlic, finely diced
1 tsp finely grated nutmeg
½ tbsp mustard powder
1 tsp sweet paprika
½ tbsp fine cracked black pepper
½ tbsp salt
175g grated sharp cheddar

175g grated mozzarella, or broken up mozzarella balls
85g grated Parmesan
2 bay leaves
2 small eggs, beaten
Panko bread crumbs
2 spring onions, chopped, for garnishing

Get me big stockpot. No, Kurwa, a *stockpot*. It's like a big saucepan. No, a *big* one. Kurwa. Fill two-thirds with water and set it to boil. Now salt well. What is that, Kurwa? We're not fucking salad bar. I said, salt it WELL. For fuck's sake: dice those onions and mince that garlic. Melt 2 tbsp of butter on lowest heat in another large stockpot for the Mornay sauce. No, a stockpot. No, a big one. Again? Really? ON THE LOWEST HEAT! Are you fucking deaf? Add minced onion and garlic once butter is melted, you are only looking to soften and not brown the onion and garlic. Kurwa. I go for smoking.

Right, where were we? Once onion and garlic are soft, remove from pot and set aside. Eh? In a fucking bowl. Kurwa. Now add 400g of butter to the stockpot and allow to melt over low heat. Jesus. Is butter melted? Good, good … now slowly whisk in plain flour a little at a time, avoiding lumps until a smooth roux is formed. Your wrist hurts? *I do not fucking care.* What? A roux? It's French. It means – just … just fucking cook it on low heat for 5 minutes, stirring occasionally. Yes, I will be for smoking. No, *you* don't have time for a fucking cigarette. I'm not paying you to fucking smoke.

Once the roux has cooked down, add back the onions, garlic and all dry spices except for salt. Now, add milk *little by little* – really, I fucking mean it, if you dump it all in at once I will come round and jam that fucking whisk right up your loading bay. Keep stirring with whisk until smooth and incorporated. Add the bay leaves to the mix. Incorporated? What am I? Fucking dictionary? By this time water for pasta should be at the boil – but you didn't turn the fucking gas on, did you? I'm going for smoke.

Boiling now? Good. Add pasta, stir once and put the lid straight back on, allowing the pasta to cook for 8 minutes or until al dente. Al dente? It means so it still has some bite. Sweet Jesus … during these 8 minutes do not sit around doing fuck-all like your mothers: *keep stirring the Mornay sauce, Kurwa*, while cook on medium heat, whisking out any lumps that form. I cannot express how little I care how much your fucking wrist hurts. Kurwa. Me? For smoking.

Once pasta done turn off and remove from heat, drain and allow it to steam. Pro tip – use a fucking colander. You! Boil more pasta. You! Tell me when done: smoking.

Moving quickly, *quickly*, go to Mornay sauce. QUICKLY, I SAID. Turn off heat – no the OTHER off – and stir in 750g of the grated cheddar BIT-BY-FUCKING-BIT until a smooth cheese sauce is formed, then add salt and stir. If I see one fucking lump I will enjoying to hurt you when I return from smoke. Sauce is smooth? Good. Now, temper a few ladles of the sauce into the eggs. Temper? Errr … Add – slowly. It means add – no, SLOWLY! Kurwa. So once the eggs are *tempered* to the sauce, add them into the rest of the sauce and stir to combine well. Now add sauce into drained pasta and stir well. Yes, I know it's heavy. No, I don't care.

Put half mixture into a deep baking tin. That is not deep enough. Bigger. Now, top with half the mozzarella – and remaining cheddar. Then add another layer of the pasta mixture and top with the remaining mozzarella, and the Parmesan. Yes, yes I know it smells like chef changing room. No, don't throw away: it's supposed to smell like that. Sprinkle with panko, cover with foil and bake in the oven on 190 °C for 30–35 minutes.

Take it out carefully – It's ho … Someone go and get fucking burn kit. So … just to clarify – THINGS COMING OUT OF OVEN ARE HOT. Can somebody please clean up all this fucking Mac 'n' Cheese off the floor. Start again. Make more. Call me when done. Errr … Guys? Does anybody have a cigarette I could borrow? Please?

YP

RED SNAPPER

A.K.A. YIANNI'S BREAKFAST

555 words (the Beast before cocktails)
Courtesy of Giles Looker / Hosted by DBC Pierre

THERE comes a time in every man's life when he must stand up and be counted. This is mine, so listen: there is no fucking reason under the sun, unless you're at the Red Ass Bar & Grill in Holeburn, Texas, for a tomato-based drink to sear the roof out of your mouth. If you grew up thinking that a Red Snapper or Bloody Mary was all about the chilli, you are wrong. If you're a bartender spreading this illusion by adding ounces of hot sauce to one of the most pleasurable and healthy pick-me-ups the world has ever known, you are a dickhead and we will hunt you down. It is not macho to destroy a drink; it is the work of a cretin.

Moreover, if you grew up thinking that these drinks go best with vodka, think again. If you are a French contributor to this myth owing to your perception of gin as something English and therefore hateful, you are a French dickhead and we will find you before the Dutch do.

Because get this: tomato juice goes best with gin. Gin has more flavour than vodka, it perfectly balances the juice, and anyway vodka's not even French so fuck them.

The whole scam arose in 1921 at the New York Bar in Paris after the French balked at using live red snappers to mix cocktails; this led to the Bloody Mary, and to the promotion of cross-Channel hatred via the suppression of gin. Why did we still liberate them during the war? I'll tell you exactly why, and it still brings a smile to my face: because their actions left them drinking an inferior drink for the rest of the fucking century. Ha! Fuck them.

If you're serious about the Red Snapper, I will give you the keys. This firm favourite at #MEATEASY became known as Yianni's Breakfast, and as a breakfast it needs to be hearty: use a large (14oz) glass, and a good thick tomato juice for best results. And note: NEVER shake tomato juice – what are you, French? Tomato juice should at most be rolled in a Boston tumbler, or simply stirred over ice in its glass. If you roll it, muddle some cucumber into the shaker for a really fresh finish; a pinch of sugar also coaxes flavour from the juice, especially if you're stuck with a cheap one. In any event, for my money I would avoid pre-seasoned juices, they're mostly over-salted and just don't have the kick. Yes, KICK – not fucking aneurysm. By all means adjust the spice to your taste, but alert us to any bartender who tries to kill you with it. Because this, my friend, is the perfect mix for a morning beverage:

35ml gin
175ml Red Snapper mix

RED SNAPPER MIX (Serves 8)
Add the following to a large jug and chill in the fridge before serving (1g = a large pinch):

100ml Worcestershire sauce
40ml Tabasco sauce
60ml pickle juice
2g celery salt
3g cayenne pepper
1g tajin (see p. 126)
1g smoked paprika
3g sugar
1g cracked black pepper
80ml lemon juice
100ml orange juice
1l tomato juice

Pour 35ml of gin into a trigger glass full of cubed ice, top with Red Snapper mix, stir, garnish with a slice of cucumber, season with black pepper and serve.

DONKEY PUNCH

Courtesy of Giles Looker

ORIGINALLY conceived at about 4 a.m. after a long night by Yianni and Josh – gatekeeper of #MEATEASY and master of the Hellhound – the Donkey Punch, a kind of bastardised Moscow Mule, has been one of the most popular drinks on the menu ever since.

WHAT YOU NEED

40ml vodka
25ml absinthe
15ml fresh lime juice
Ginger beer

WHAT YOU DO

Add the absinthe to a tall 12oz glass. Swill it around so it coats the inside of the glass and pour the excess back into the spirit measure.

Fill the glass with cubed ice. Build the vodka and fresh lime over the ice, topping with ginger beer.

Add a couple of drops of the reserved absinthe to the top of the drink before serving.

Garnish with a wedge of lime. DRINK.

MORNING GLORY

IN MEMORY OF SCOTCH BOBBY

Courtesy of Giles Looker

BOBBY was a legend. One of his last bar shifts on this earth was at the #MEATEASY where he was a resident on the jars. He was one of the good guys and also made some of the best drinks ever tasted. Always wore a smile and had a drink up his sleeve or in his hand. No one could understand a word that came out of his mouth due to his strong Glaswegian accent. Anyone who got served by Bobby always remembered him, even the harshest food critics often namechecked him on his exceptional service and drinks.

This is one of Bobby's greats.

WHAT YOU NEED

20ml Bowmore 12 yr
½ bar spoon of orange marmalade
5ml Gran Marnier
10ml lemon juice
Champagne

WHAT YOU DO

Take the first 4 ingredients and place into a cocktail shaker
Add cubed ice and shake.

Pour into a champagne flute and top with champagne.
DRINK.

CORPSE REVIVERS

Courtesy of Giles Looker

I INTRODUCED the Corpse Reviver to Yianni and Josh at the #MEATEASY in the first couple of weeks it was open. It seemed like the perfect drink for them, as it's the best hair of the dog going. Originally made by grave diggers in Slough, the Corpse Reviver was made famous by Harry Craddock in his 1930 *Savoy Cocktail Book*. There are several different recipes, and the number depends on the spirit. The version made for the boys on that ill-fated night was the Corpse Reviver No. 2.

CORPSE REVIVER NO. 2

15ml gin
15ml lemon juice
15ml Cointreau
15ml Kina Lillet
A dash of absinthe

Take all ingredients and place in a Boston shaker. Add cubed ice and shake.

Strain into a chilled 7oz cocktail glass and DRINK.

After several of these, the drink became a little too sweet and they wanted a drier finish, just so they could consume more of them. Out of nowhere came the bright idea to drop Kina Lillet and replace it with absinthe, with champagne to top. A drink was born … the Corpse Reviver No. 69.

CORPSE REVIVER NO. 69
(for normal people)

15ml gin
15ml absinthe
15ml Cointreau
15ml lemon juice
Champagne to top

Take the first 4 ingredients and place in a Boston shaker. Add cubed ice and shake.

Strain into a chilled 7oz cocktail glass, top with champagne and DRINK.

IRENA'S REVIVER
(put away all sharp objects)

This is the drink that Yianni and Josh insisted on drinking constantly and is also the reason why memories of the #MEATEASY are so vague. The gin was removed and replaced with more absinthe creating a stronger, even drier drink.

25ml absinthe
15ml Cointreau
15ml Kina Lillet
15ml lemon juice
Champagne to top

Take the first 4 ingredients and place in a Boston shaker. Add cubed ice and shake the fuck out of it.

Strain into a chilled 7oz cocktail glass, top with champagne and HOLD ON TIGHT.

THE NEGRONI

Courtesy of Giles Looker

THE Negroni is often seen as a drink only ordered by old people, hipsters and bartenders. The story goes that this mix of gin, Campari and sweet vermouth was invented at Bar Casoni in Florence around 1920, when one regular, Count Camillo Negroni, asked for his Americano (Campari, sweet vermouth and soda water) to be made with gin and no soda. Pro-American goodwill in the wake of World War I had established the Americano as the most fashionable cocktail, but once Casoni customers started ordering their Americanos 'the Negroni way', a classic was born.

WHAT YOU NEED

25ml gin
25ml sweet vermouth
25ml Campari

GARNISH
Orange slice

WHAT YOU DO

Place all ingredients into a rocks glass over cubed ice and stir. DRINK.

THE NEW CROSS NEGRONI

Courtesy of Giles Looker

THE New Cross Negroni was one of the few house cocktails we had on the menu at #MEATEASY, it is our version of the classic (if not better). Instead of using equal parts gin, Campari and sweet vermouth we went gin heavy and used a lighter Italian liqueur, Aperol (which is perfect for Spritz also) and a heavier, full-bodied Italian vermouth, Antica Formula. The sweetness, bitterness and punch of gin is a killer combination and makes for a great aperitif or six.

WHAT YOU NEED

35ml Tanqueray gin
15ml Antica Formula
20ml Aperol

GARNISH
Orange twist

WHAT YOU DO

Place all ingredients into a rocks glass over cubed ice and stir. Express the orange twist over the cocktail. DRINK.

THE SAZERAC

Courtesy of Giles Looker

A NEW Orleans cocktail through and through and the perfect drink for every occasion, the Sazerac came about around the time of 1850 from a chap by the name of Swell T. Taylor who gave up his Merchants Exchange Coffee House (a bar) in New Orleans and went on to import booze. One of his brands was a cognac named Sazerac de Forge et Fils. At this time Aaron Bird, a clerk, took over the Merchant Exchange and changed the name to the Sazerac House – its speciality was the 'Sazerac cocktail', a drink made with Taylor's Sazerac cognac and, it's claimed, bitters made down the road by a pharmacist by the name Anonie Amedie Peychaud. Peychaud's Bitters are still used widely in cocktails and can be bought at specialist shops.

Over the years cognac was used less and rye whiskey or bourbon was called for. All three make a damn fine drink so I leave it up to you to choose.

WHAT YOU NEED

60ml bourbon/rye/cognac
5ml sugar syrup
1 dash Peychaud's Bitters
1 dash Angustura Bitters
5ml absinthe

GARNISH
Orange and lemon twist

WHAT YOU DO

Take a pre-chilled rocks glass, add 5ml of absinthe and throw the glass as high as you can in the air, spinning it so that it is washed with the absinthe. Then place back in the fridge/freezer.

Take a mixing glass, add cubed ice and pour the rest of the ingredients into it. Stir.

Once the drink is chilled and diluted strain the liquid into the pre-chilled, absinthe-washed glass.

This drink is served with no ice. Express both of the twists over the drink, leaving the orange twist in the glass, and serve. DRINK.

BLOOD & SAND

Courtesy of Giles Looker

BLOOD oranges mostly come from Mediterranean countries (southern Italy in particular). The two most popular varieties are the dark-fleshed Moro, which are available from December to March, and the Tarocco, from January to May. We were lucky enough to get a few weeks of the most perfect blood oranges while the #MEATEASY was open and so we thought it only appropriate to dedicate a drink to this beautiful fruit. For the next two to three weeks the whole bar drank Blood & Sand, with fresh blood-orange juice (the sand).

The Blood & Sand is one of the great classic whisky cocktails. It first appeared in *The Savoy Cocktail Book* by Harry Craddock in 1930. No one really knows who came up with the drink but it is believed to have been created for the film premiere of the 1922 film *Blood and Sand* starring Rudolph Valentino.

It's a great drink made even better by using these delicious oranges.

WHAT YOU NEED

25ml whisky
25ml sweet vermouth
25ml Cherry Heering
25ml blood-orange juice

GARNISH
Orange twist

WHAT YOU DO

Place all the ingredients into a cocktail shaker and shake.

Pour ingredients into a pre-chilled cocktail glass, garnish and DRINK.

✝

THE LAST POST

LAST Sunday night we killed #MEATEASY. After three months of meat-sweats and absinthe, we shut it down in the most fitting way possible. At our Drink the Bar Dry party just 150 people went through:

Two and a half grand's worth of booze
Fifteen hundred quid's worth of curry
Two dozen #MEATEASY tattoos
One stripper
A wide assortment of splintered furniture
Three doors
One ambulance call
Two police visits

Well done, everybody.

Job done.

#MEATEASY R.I.P.

HUEY MORGAN

1. AND THE CRADLE WILL ROCK –
   VAN HALEN
2. HIGHWAY TO HELL – AC/DC
3. WE WILL ROCK YOU – QUEEN
4. NO QUARTER – LED ZEPPELIN
5. PARANOID – BLACK SABBATH
6. HOLD THE LINE – TOTO
7. TUSH – ZZ TOP
8. MY WOMAN FROM TOKYO –
   DEEP PURPLE
9. BORN TO RUN – BRUCE SPRINGSTEEN
10. BAD REPUTATION – THIN LIZZY
11. TAKE THE LONG WAY HOME –
    SUPERTRAMP
12. TAKIN' IT TO THE STREETS –
    DOOBIE BROTHERS
13. BABA O'RILEY – THE WHO

HOGS, HIPPIES & HUMDINGERS

EXODUS

THE MEATliquor CHRONICLES
PART FIVE

222 words (not a Beast, a calibre)

THE FEEDING OF THE FAITHFUL

IT CAN happen, when returning to a path in life from a detour around some obstacle, that the places you pass on the detour lie further ahead on your chosen path. Many old women have spoken of blessings in disguise, and in essence speak of this; but the secret mathematics of it speak also of righteousness and power. They say that certain spirits honestly called to an idea are actually called to Quality and to Truth. They are not the madcaps forever planning a pork butchery in Kabul but the few sensitive enough to taste Quality in its raw form, wherever they find it – and capable of sniffing it through a contrary breeze. In this condition, when they deploy their energies, they create their own following wind.

A following wind like this is a kind of destiny because it always blows on-course, behind their passion. Thus, in the salon which misfortune made the MEATdaddy borrow, without wheels, a kind of church, the first one, he was able to gather strength and launch new wheels, feeding the 5,000 who massed sober and hungry on the land.

And he also saw the future – a permanent church.

It took Christians over 200 years to sort a church. The legion of three did it within a year.

Well, a training church.

DBC

✝

ONE MAN AND HIS HOG

By Bates

BEING from South Carolina there ain't no need to have a special occasion to have a hog roast – any ol' Saturday will do. My Granddaddy raised hogs amongst most everything else he raised to eat so I suppose that's where my love of swine comes from. Hog roasting is a learned skill passed down from greater pot-bellied men than myself that took me many hogs to master. I've spent 13 years in restaurant kitchens and still hate hearing chefs refer to their trade as an 'art', but in the case of pit cooking I have a hard time thinking of it as anything but an 'art'. Keeping a careful eye on the coals, knowing where and when to move them, getting that meat fork-tender over many hours without burning or crisping up the skin too soon. I ain't saying I'm a hog whisperer but I'm damn sure close.

A hog, a hole, wood, basting mop and loads of time. These five things come together to make something much greater than the sum of their parts. I've been cooking animals over fire since I was knee high to a June bug and it's still hands down my favourite form of cooking. You don't need any special equipment, just know-how. I've cobbled pits out of fencing, scaffolding, rebar – hell, you name it, I've used it. It's certainly not the easiest way of cooking. In fact, I couldn't think of anything much more time intensive and laborious than cooking a whole hog. Digging a pit by hand, chopping a truck-bed-ful of wood, moving cinder blocks and whatever manner of cooking apparatus you've fashioned out of your begging, borrowing or (ahem) stealing endeavours. Shit, just the lugging and moving around of a whole pig carcass sheds new light for you on why people get caught with bodies in their backyard – ain't nothing simple about hauling about 200lb of dead weight. Despite or perhaps because of all of this hard work the rewards are tremendous and will probably be the only time you can get your layabout buddies to put in an honest day's work. It's amazing, the seductive powers of roast pork and booze.

It goes without saying there is something primal about digging a pit, lighting a fire and setting a whole animal upon it to cook all night. Slowly mopping the hog and tending the fire with a couple of friends, music playing and beers being sipped, waiting for the hog to turn a deep, crisp auburn on the outside, the meat falling apart on the inside. Greeting the sun with a bleary-eyed bourbon-induced haze, hoping to catch a few hours' sleep before the party, knowing you'll probably just drink on through before the first folks arrive for the humdinger. So you pull up your bootstraps and stop being a bitch about things. You're in the home stretch. All that hard work and hard drinking, hours of caressing and moving coals to the right spot at just the right degree of Satan's asshole – don't fuck it up now. Crank those coals and get that hog flipped over to bubble and crisp all that glistening skin. This is when the partygoers start milling around you, swilling their beers, mesmerised by the beauty of so much fat, muscle, heat and time. Asking such foolhardy things as 'Could I get just a piece of that crackling?' No, you rube, you can't – this is my time to shine. You can wait like all the others, and wait you will make them do. Because it's in that last hour of cooking that you pour into everyone else's soul the agonising time and work that's gone into this hog – the anticipation of greasy fingers, fat-smeared mouths, guts laden with meat, booze, revelry and lust trying to shovel in just one more mouthful of all four. You stretch out that hour so it seems to everyone to be an entire night, a night soaked in liquor and lies of grand tales, of dreams and failures, jokes and reminiscence, a night built of the shit mankind has been doing for millennia – the kill, the fire, the cook. All culminating in a moment that links us still to our ancestors as you and your crew lay that hog on the table for everyone to devour and for that brief moment you are GOD.

So bring your coolers of beer, bottles of bourbon, friends and kin – we're having a pig pickin'.

LONDON LAMB CHOPS

LAMB cooked over hot coals holds a special place in my heart: from turning the spit in the merciless midday sun as a child in Greece to stuffing myself full of the lamb lollipops at Tayyabs in East London. At #MEATEASY we served these a couple of times, cooked out the front of the pub over a small charcoal mangal. The spicing is pure South London – a mongrel mixture of Mediterranean and Asian flavours and techniques. Cook 'em pink and revel in the mess!

YP

WHAT YOU NEED

2–4 lamb chops per person

FOR THE MARINADE
2 inches fresh ginger (peeled)
4 cloves garlic (peeled)
4 green chillies (seeds removed)
1 pinch salt
1 tsp hot chilli powder
1 tsp ground cumin
1 tsp ground coriander
1 tsp ground cinnamon
1 tsp turmeric
1 lemon (juice and zest)
3 tbsp full-fat Greek yogurt

WHAT YOU DO

Blend the ginger, garlic, chillies and salt with a little water until it becomes a paste.

Place the chops into a large bowl and add the paste, rubbing well into the meat.

Add the lemon juice and zest, rubbing well into the meat.

Combine the dry spices with the yogurt and pour over the chops. Work the sauce into the meat until every chop has a good covering.

Cover with cling film and allow to sit for at least two hours.

Grill under a medium heat for 15 minutes turning once, making sure that they become golden but do not burn.

Before serving, sprinkle with freshly squeezed lemon juice. Serve with a cucumber and mint tzatziki.

NAME: Eleni
DRINK: no shots
MEMORY: hazy

CYDER CAR

Courtesy of Giles Looker

THIS cocktail is a combination of two drinks that go together like Adam and Eve.

CIDER

I was first introduced to proper cider at Glastonbury Festival in my early raving years. Back then we were all a little short of money and we were always on the hunt for the cheapest alcoholic fix. I remember quite clearly one late night/early morning, feeling somewhat thirsty, a good friend of mine suggested we take a walk up to the Green Fields for some local brew. After an hour's walk through the mud we arrived at his favourite hippy watering hole. We were the only people at the small tent and were invited to have a seat, then were presented with a flagon of homemade cider each. It was a fantastic balance of dry and sweet and crisp, with a refreshing hit of apple, but most of all it was highly alcoholic. This is one of my most memorable drinking moments at any festival, as we watched the sun come up over Glastonbury. This is the morning I fell in love with cider.

SIDE CAR

The Side Car first appears in Harry MacElhone's book *ABC of Mixing Cocktails*. It first appeared on a cocktail list at the Ritz Hotel in Paris. It is easily one of the best classic cocktails ever made, and is still shaken and served in all great bars today. It is brandy shaken with Cointreau and fresh lemon juice served straight up in a cocktail glass with a sugared rim.

The Cyder Car takes the best bits of both drinks and puts them into one long glass.

WHAT YOU NEED

35ml Somerset brandy
15ml Cointreau
15ml lemon juice
10ml sugar syrup
85ml West Country cider

GARNISH
A slice of apple and lemon each

WHAT YOU DO

Take the first 4 ingredients and place into a cocktail shaker. Add ice and shake vigorously.

Strain out the ingredients into a 12oz tall glass over cubed ice.

Top with chilled cider.

Garnish and DRINK.

The Cyder Car can also be served warmed.

BACKYARD BURGER

IN THE course of my travels across the USA, I've seen many different methods of preparing and cooking burgers, and in general the simpler recipes work best on a barbecue (our transatlantic cousins would call it a grill).

This technique of using a thick, circular slice of onion is a classic serving method in roadside burger joints all over the States. In most cases the onion would be raw, but for this recipe we're going to cook it a bit on the barbecue, sweetening and softening the onion so it doesn't overpower the meat.

I always use processed American-style cheese slices. I don't use them for anything else, but on a burger no other cheese comes close.

For the bun, use a white roll with a bit of texture. It needs to be able to stand up to the meat juices without disintegrating.

Your butcher will be happy to grind you some chuck steak, ideally something dry-aged.

You'll also need a barbecue and some real charcoal. Try and get hold of some British hardwood charcoal – you get a much better flavour than you do with briquettes.

YP

WHAT YOU NEED

160g freshly ground chuck steak
A generous pinch of salt and pepper
1 burger bun
A half-inch-thick slice of a large white onion
2 slices of American-style cheese
A squirt of Heinz ketchup
A similarly sized squirt of French's mustard
2 or 3 slices of dill pickle (not the sweet ones)

WHAT YOU DO

Light your charcoal, preferably with a chimney starter rather than chemical fire starters. The coals will need to burn down to cooking temperature. Be patient: this will take a while. When the coals are coated with a white ash (they will glow red in the dark) and all the flames have died down, you're ready to cook.

Pull out a wad of ground chuck steak and form it into a ball with your hands. Squash this down onto a sheet of greaseproof paper so that it forms a burger patty. It should be a bit bigger than the bun to allow for shrinkage during cooking.

Place the patty on an oiled and preheated barbecue grill and cover the top side with a healthy dose of salt and pepper. Put the thick slice of onion on the barbecue, too.

Meanwhile, cut the bun in half and toast the cut sides over the barbecue. This will only take a few seconds. When the bottom of the burger has formed a good brown crust, it will easily lift off the barbecue without sticking. Flip it and cook the other side. It won't take nearly as long. Flip the onion when it starts to brown.

Lay a couple of slices of 'cheese' over the burger while it's on the barbecue.

Squirt some Heinz ketchup and French's mustard on the bottom of the bun. Stick a couple of slices of dill pickle on there.

Lay the burger onto your bun base and stack the onion on top. Put the bun lid on top and serve immediately.

Drink: something with an umbrella.

YIANNI

1. LAWYERS, GUNS AND MONEY -
WARREN ZEVON

2. VOODOO CHILD (SLIGHT RETURN) -
THE JIMI HENDRIX EXPERIENCE

3. I WANNA BE YOUR DOG - THE STOOGES

4. BLITZKRIEG BOP - RAMONES

5. DANCE LIKE A MONKEY -
NEW YORK DOLLS

6. EVER FALLEN IN LOVE
(WITH SOMEONE YOU SHOULDN'T'VE)? -
BUZZCOCKS

7. FUNNEL OF LOVE - THE FALL

8. TOO DRUNK TO FUCK - DEAD KENNEDYS

9. HILLGRASS BLUEBILLY -
LEFT LANE CRUISER

10. BACON MARTINI -
WHISKEY DAREDEVILS

11. IT'S SO EASY - GUNS N' ROSES

12. BRING YOUR DAUGHTER...
TO THE SLAUGHTER - IRON MAIDEN

13. ACE OF SPADES - MOTÖRHEAD

THE LESSON OF THE TEMPLE

THE MEATliquor CHRONICLES
PART SIX

333 words (the sawn-off Beast)

'SURELY your gospels, and all they represent, must live in the air?' a layperson said to the MEATdaddy. 'Because the qualities you celebrate in this place are around us at all times – they're enlightenments, decisions, forces that resist herding into cathedrals like this. I mean, didn't the mobile gospels prove more apt, in that the wagon exposed itself to a greater volume of what we seek? Wasn't it better that diverse peoples from all around came at the wagon's appearance, rather than to one unmoving place?'

'My fellow: you are right and wrong. While it's true that what we celebrate here is ultimately intangible, an alloy of spirit that springs from one remaining instinct among many that have withered, an instinct towards Quality, itself withered and gone from the masses – this cathedral is built for revellers, who are tangible. It's for them who capture and amplify the thing you describe, and because they are tangible this is a place for them to gather which doesn't move, so they know where to find it again.'

'No, well,' said the layperson, 'you describe them as tangible; but if what they gather to focus upon is a protocol of choices according to a value system, like any other system, including the opposite one – then by nature, whether you colour it with religion or logic, your Unique Selling Point is just a value. If all I carry into the cathedral is an intangible value, and if it consumes my whole purpose in going there, then I become intangible too, for the purposes of argument. And as intangible, I need go nowhere, because the value I represent can be argued in my absence.'

The MEATdaddy took a moment to adjust his robes, examining the well-worn sole of a sandal. 'Except for one thing,' he said: 'a burger and a cocktail are tangible.'

'Ah: but then …'

'Do you want a fucking burger or not?'

'I mean …'

'Fuck off, there's a queue forming.'

'Eh?'

'We don't serve intangibles.'

DBC

A Place of Worship was builded there

✝

CANS V. BOTTLES

By Ben McFarland

FOR years, the beer can has been viewed as the village idiot of vessels, its head pompously patted by haughty craft-beer connoisseurs as if it were a grinning smudge-faced simpleton who points at planes and dribbles down his front.

But this perception of the can as a plebeian package is completely misplaced. The classic aluminium can is the ideal container in which to house one's high-quality hooch. So long synonymous with mass-produced moribund swill hawked by marketing men, it's quick becoming the sealed container of choice for contemporary craft brewers.

When compared to glass bottles, the case for cans is a compelling one. Cans don't break, they're lighter than bottles and take up less space, they're more environmentally friendly, easier to transport and, let's face it, they look a lot sexier too.

But, more crucially, the can is simply better for the beer inside, keeping it consistently fresher and flavoursome for longer. While bottle-conditioned beers, vintage ales and more esoteric styles like Lambic evolve and improve with age, the vast majority of beer is designed to be drunk in as fresh a condition as possible.

For beer to be kept fresh, it needs to be protected from its two arch-enemies: sunlight and oxygen. Cans are much better at doing that than bottles. Oxygen is ruinous to beer and, from the mash to the packaging hall, brewers do everything they can to keep it out.

Oxygen tends to open an almighty can of whuppass on beer, reacting with elements within to create off-putting, stale notes and tastes akin to wet cardboard, leather and lipstick.

While it's virtually impossible to avoid any oxygen pick-up at all during the brewing and packaging of the beer, modern canning processes drastically reduce it by filling the hermetically sealed, flat-topped can with CO_2 and letting in very little oxygen at all.

Beer doesn't like light either. Exposure to UV light can render it 'light-struck', making it taste funny – but not in an amusing way. When exposed to light for extended periods of time, compounds found in hops unleash an unpleasant aroma that white-coated boffins call MBT or '3-methyl-2-butene-1-thiol'.

More colloquially referred to as 'skunk-like', it's very similar in scent to the notorious stench sprayed from the anal glands of said stripy mammals. This is not something brewers tend to put on their bottle labels but perhaps they should because clear or green (and even brown to a lesser extent) glass bottles offer little protection to the harmful effects of light.

Cans, however, are completely impermeable to such ruinous rays. We've looked into it, quite literally, and we can confirm that it's very dark inside a beer can. Seriously.

A criticism often made of cans in the past was that they tainted the beer with a metallic 'off' flavour. This is partly because beer in a can back then tended to be lousy beer, brewed badly and blemished with an array of unwanted oxidised flavours – one of which would have been 'metallic'.

Also, back in the 1980s, canning technology was far more rudimentary than it is today and the beer would have come into direct contact with the can. Now, however, cans are lined with a very thin, über-sophisticated impenetrable polymer coating that prevents the beer touching or tasting of the metal.

Perceptions of canned beer are, slowly but surely, changing. Just as winemakers overcame scepticism of the screwcap or 'Stelvin closure', a growing number of brewers and discerning drinkers are realising that canned craft beer is the future.

More than a decade after Oskar Blues became the first microbrewer in America to embrace the beer can as his principal packaging, another 250 microbreweries have followed suit. According to the latest count, there are now more than 725 craft beers available in cans, covering approximately 80 different beer styles ranging from fruit beers and stouts to imperial porters, from wheat beers brewed using watermelon to oak-aged Belgian-style abbey ales brewed with figs and vanilla beans.

Britain, however, has found itself slightly behind the canned craft-beer curve. The first canned craft beer exclusively available in the UK was Hobo, a Bohemian Pilsner-style lager brewed with 100 per cent Saaz hops, matured for two months and fermented in open squares at the Žatec Brewery in the Czech Republic, the birthplace of golden lagers.

So, just because your first canned beer was lousy doesn't mean all canned beer is bad. Quite the contrary, canned beer is the future. It's like the Internet.

Unlike bottled beers, canned craft brews can be drunk at any time, in any place, and you don't need to carry a bottle opener or break your teeth to do so. You can take them to the beach where they won't cut the feet of little children or endanger innocent sea life. Recent research revealed that empty bottled beers regularly get jammed in the blowholes of innocent dolphins. True story.

That simply doesn't happen with cans.

✞

NO RESERVATIONS

A DRUNKEN DISCUSSION

Refereed by Stefan Chomka,
with an Afterthought by Grace Dent

RESTAURANTS that don't take bookings and instead expect their customers to wait in the cold for an available table are opportunistic money-grabbers of the lowest kind. And those people that queue are no more than a mindless set of trend-chasing fools with more time than brain cells to kill.

That's, at least, what the media would have you believe, given the furore a handful of restaurants that don't take reservations has caused over the last few years. 'How can such places expect to have loyal customers?' they decry, and 'What a blatant lack of respect for the paying patron.' If you happen to have the misfortune to stumble across a no-booking restaurant, dear reader, a brick through the window is an acceptable course of action, is their general (if often unwritten) message.

For a nation quick to deride the Germans for putting their towels out early on sunbeds we're more than happy to do the same when it comes to eating out. First come first served might be the protocol at the poolside in Playa de las Americas but it certainly isn't for people eating in London restaurants, who are more than happy to put down a metaphorical towel at a table six months in the future.

Yet there's nothing more democratic about giving everybody the chance to eat at a restaurant on any given day, and dispensing with the need for customers to set an alarm clock and then repeatedly hit redial on the phone to get a booking at somewhere they genuinely want to eat. If you've ever queued to get into MEATliquor, or Polpo, Pitt Cue, Burger & Lobster or any of the other restaurants whose access isn't restricted by the tyranny of the early booker, the hyper-efficient PA or the international gastro-tourist that has meals mapped out eight months in advance, we salute you and your patience. There are reasons we do what we do, and those reasons are outlined here.

Of course, not all queues – and queuers – are equal. Those dullards who pitch a tent outside an Apple Store five days before the next colour of iPad is launched. They can do one.

THE CAST

JAMIE BERGER
After reading Chinese at Cambridge and trying his hand at investment banking, Berger went on to complete a PhD at Harvard University. When it comes to barbecuing food you can never be overqualified, however; and when he's not trying to teach business partner Tom Adams Mandarin he's working the room at his barbecue restaurant Pitt Cue.

TOM ADAMS
The co-founder of Pitt Cue was working as a chef de partie under Jeremy Lee at the Blueprint Café when he decided to open a trailer serving barbecue food as a bit of holiday fun. The snaking queues at the van, located under Hungerford Bridge on London's South Bank, eventually encouraged Adams to become a full-time barbecue man and he hasn't looked back. Alongside partner Jamie Berger he opened the 30-seater no reservations restaurant just off Carnaby Street in January 2012.

RUSSELL NORMAN
Once described by the *Observer* as 'a man with a licence to thrill', Norman was Operations Director at Caprice Holdings – owner of the Ivy, Scott's and J. Sheekey – before becoming a restaurateur proper with the launch of Polpo in Soho in 2009. His New York-inspired Venetian-style bacaro, complete with small plates, low-hanging Edison light bulbs and a no-bookings policy, was a zeitgeist-grabbing idea that has since spawned numerous interpretations across the country.

DAVID STRAUSS

When the Operations Director of Russian-owned Goodman Restaurants isn't juggling the eight tonnes of live lobster his company imports every week or how to manage the lines of people queuing outside his Burger & Lobster restaurants he's watching football, eating steak, spreading his infectious brand of positivity, and being bullied by Scott and Yianni.

YOUR NAME'S NOT DOWN

YIANNI PAPOUTSIS: I never thought queuing would become an issue. I walk past a hundred pubs every Friday night where I'd like a pint but I can't because they're full. I just find somewhere else. I don't start abusing the owners on social media because they're busy.

RUSSELL NORMAN: I never wanted people to queue at Polpo or Spuntino. I wanted a place where you could walk in and sit straight down. I noticed very early on at Polpo that we took bookings and were massively oversubscribed. Every evening hundreds of very cool Soho types came through the door and said, 'Hi there, table for two,' and it broke my heart to say to these guys that were fully booked. We were turning away our long-term customers and taking bookings from people who come once only to see what all the fuss was about. That had to change. We honoured the bookings we'd taken two weeks in advance, took no further bookings, and that was it. Within two weeks we stopped being a restaurant that took bookings.

JAMIE BERGER: We're an 18-seat restaurant in a high-rent area. I don't think we're guilty by not taking reservations.

RN: A restaurant that doesn't take reservations should not be defined by this one aspect of its operation. When I hear people talk about 'no-reservation restaurants' it seems as odd to me as someone saying 'no-music restaurants' or 'no-linen-napkin restaurants'. Our places should be defined by what they serve, how they serve it and the environment in which they serve it, not by something as mundane and incidental as the way they seat customers.

TOM ADAMS: We just want to serve delicious food. You shouldn't have to take reservations to do this.

RN: The experience at Polpo starts with the queue. Our regular customers know the score, that it's a neighbourhood restaurant and that we don't take bookings. They're also intelligent and know that if they don't want to wait two hours they come early or late. If they do come at 8 p.m. they know they have to wait an hour and a half but they also know they're going to have a few drinks while they wait. When they sit down they are well oiled and have a great evening.

SCOTT COLLINS: Then you've got a restaurant full of people who are like-minded.

YP: If you want to come to one of our restaurants you can go there tonight. You do not have to arrange a holiday in six months' time for a booking.

RN: If you book Janet's birthday party for 4 September and spend the whole summer looking forward to it you can only be disappointed.

DO YOU HAVE TO LET THEM LINGER?

TA: If we have a table of five or six they are inevitably going to take longer but they are the people who on Friday and Saturday night create that buzz in a restaurant. And if they are still drinking there's no need to pressure them to leave.

JB: We have nothing that is conducive to lingering. We serve wine by the glass not the bottle, there's no hot drinks, no Wi-Fi.

SC: I've never noticed how shit you are …

YP: We have the same problem with desserts. We get a table of six in and one person wants a dessert. That person will linger on that dessert in the time it would take to turn the table, thereby making the queue longer.

RUNNING A QUEUE

DAVID STRAUSS: You can have your moment in the sunshine but in ten years' time there might be a backlash about restaurants that leave their customers standing in a queue. Burger & Lobster might have a two-hour queue, but if you don't treat the queue properly in two years' time you haven't got one at all.

YP: We spend as much time as possible managing the queue to reduce the time people spend in it. We do absolutely everything we can to make queuing better. Our ideal, without rushing anybody, as soon as someone has properly left the table is that we can get another table seated in 45 seconds.

JB: The queuing system has to be no exceptions, everyone has to queue. If it's fair and everyone knows, that's fine. If they think that people are pushing in it's never going to work. We only take full groups onto our list and they can't leave or the name goes off the list.

DS: We're all pro-queue, but none of us will stand in one.

SC: I would. I've queued at Bone Daddies and even the manager was queuing with his boyfriend because he couldn't jump the queue.

YP: I never really queue because I just don't go at busy times. We are the only culture in Europe where everybody eats at the same time. In London, people don't want to go home and come back to eat; they want to come out of work, eat and go home.

RN: I always queue at Spuntino.

YP: I will not go through the front door of our own restaurants if there's a queue.

JB: If I want to eat at Pitt Cue I have to queue. It's very good PR to be in my queue.

RN: I was at the Spotted Pig in New York – which doesn't take reservations – having a drink with Ken [Friedman, the owner]. He was boasting about Bill Clinton coming there a lot. 'But Ken,' I said, 'the Spotted Pig doesn't take reservations, what happens with Clinton?' 'We book a table for him and we take him through,' he said. So I asked him what his regular customers say as they stand there and watch him being whisked through. [With faux

New York accent] 'I'll tell you what I say, "He used to be the fucking president of the United fucking States." '

YP: The A list will not only happily queue, they won't even try and book a table. However, the people who have been on TV for 25 seconds expect not to queue. They say, 'Do you know what kind of exposure you're going to get and you're missing out on?' [grimaces, downs a whisky]

CRITICISM

JB: People were used to queuing at the Pitt Cue truck but we get much more shit from them for having to queue at the restaurant.

YP: [Times restaurant critic] Giles Coren said we'd never have regulars because of our queues but we have hundreds. They just know when to come. From 2.00 to 5.30 p.m. we have seats at the bar where you can eat, and all our regulars come then. Or after 10.00 p.m.

RN: Do you know how many restaurants there are in London? About 12,500. And I would guess maybe 50 don't take reservations. I think it is incredibly telling that in lower Manhattan and Brooklyn nearly all the places I want to go to don't take reservations and there is never a single grumble. It is accepted that these are neighbourhood joints and they operate for the benefit of the neighbourhood.

THE CUSTOMER

RN: My ideal customer is someone who decided to come to Polpo about five minutes before they turn up.

YP: The biggest spenders on walk-ins are City Boys.

SC: City Boys makes it sound a bit derogatory. I like City Boys.

RN: We don't like them at all. I'd say 80% of our customers are female.

SC: I'm hanging out at yours.

RN: The three Polpos are massively female; there are a lot of single guys at Spuntino.

JB: We find the people who come in suits have a sense of entitlement. They are very awkward to deal with in the queue and they refuse to understand the policy. They also have a preconceived notion of how a queue should work and get unpleasant when it doesn't conform to their views.

YP: We have one City company and every Friday they have a rolling order of 80 takeaway burgers. So when we open we've already done 80 burgers.

RN: Eight zero? Can I have their phone number?

DS: The ones that get shitty are the ones you don't want to eat there anyway.

BOOKINGS AND NO-SHOWS

DS: There's nothing that bad about reservations if they turn up on time, spend money and behave properly – that's how we build businesses. I'd imagine that Tom will end up opening up a restaurant that will serve the type of wine that he likes. The only way that you'll be able to survive then is by finding people who are going to want to buy those wines and they may want to make reservations.

YP: MEATmission has two separate rooms that lend themselves to being used in two different ways. We listened to our customers and we changed our policy to meet people's requests. A lot of people were saying that they wanted to be able to come and experience what we do and make a reservation so we responded to that.

SC: But we now have a nightmare with reservations. We're trying to keep everyone happy but our level of no-shows is amazing.

YP: We get groups of 20 who have booked up in advance that are no-shows and then we get grief from queuing people looking at an empty table. Between last Friday night and Sunday we've had in excess of 100 no-shows, including two tables of 20.

SP: We all want to serve as many customers as we possibly can, but how's the best way to go about it? What we turn over in tables couldn't be achieved with reservations.

AFTERTHOUGHT

GRACE DENT
Restaurant Critic, *Evening Standard*

Boys. Oh boys. I do not queue for dinner. The only time I might queue for dinner is after an apocalyptic natural disaster post-UN helicopter drop. Quite plainly, anyone who queues for a beef burger needs to spend more downtime trying to lose their virginity. And any man who takes a date to a no-reservation bear pit so they can both be jostled about in some vile 'holding' pen deserves to die alone in a house full of pizza boxes, dubious crusty socks and keepsake napkins from your restaurants.

Democratising? More free tables? Obviously, I wholly comprehend your reasons for eschewing customer convenience and loyalty to chase any passing bum on seat. Nothing wrong with that. I love money too. But when I'm pondering dinner next Tuesday, frankly, your year-on-year financial projection is not my concern. I'm sure City Boys – who know the cost of everything and the value of nothing – love your concept. City Boys also like harlequin pattern braces and catching clap from emaciated Russian hookers. I'll eat wherever they don't.

And keeping in mind that not one of you would put up on a regular basis with the manner of front-of-house service you deliver, I hope – in a lovely, snuggly way – you all burn in hell, with a rumbling stomach, standing in a drafty corridor, being repetitively hit on the elbow by a front door and patronised by some drunk-on-power gonk who failed all her GCSEs in 2010, informing you there's nothing now but you could wait fifty-five minutes. Mazel tov!

✝

THE TRIPLE CHILI CHALLENGE

By Will Dean

'FEAR has its use but cowardice has none.' Not my words, chum, but those of Mohandas Karamchand Gandhi, a man who you suspect might not quite have had the stomach for the MEATliquor Triple Chili Challenge. Mainly because of the beef. Gandhi was pretty hard like that.

Anyway, welcome to MEATmission on the evening of 2 March in the year 2013. Where, in about 35 minutes' time, the restaurant's charming proprietor will be pushing a young man's head into the half-eaten remains of a dish of Chili Cheese Fries while a Burgerette called Holly shouts, 'You're fucking pathetic, you're a disappointment to your mother,' into a near-reputable journalist's left lughole. Lovely. And also correct.

It's not just him (alright, me) being punished. We're here for the grand finale, sort of, of the Triple Chili Challenge.

The Triple Chili Challenge has been on the menu since #MEATEASY opened. This bacchanalian protein soak involves contenders attempting to eat MEAT's Chili Dog, Chili Cheese Fries and Green Chili Cheeseburger in less than ten minutes. And although it's not like one of those grim *Man v. Food* challenges where the contender has to eat his or her own bodyweight in turducken in 47 seconds, it's not easy.

If you complete the TCC you get your grub courtesy of the angry-looking Greek man stood at the pass. Fail and, well, son, you're a failure. And you have to pay for your food. And the four pints of Grog you needed to wash it down. Tough luck, bozo.

It's a play-off reserved for MEATliquor's most masochistic customers. But also a play-off reserved for a handful of absolute winners for whom the idea of downing a metric shit-tonne of mince is not even in the slightest bit of a big deal.

In celebration of these maniacs, three of the all-time fastest TCCers have been invited back to see if they could repeat their heroics on the competitive stage. Sadly, one of them is some kind of Japanese extreme eating contestant who's just gone back to Fukuoka to snort bits of whale. So a boo-hooing journalist has been invited to test his stomach instead. Great.

The other two TCC all-stars do turn up, though. First is Andrew, a sturdy North-Easterner, who's followed by Nick, an Australian built like a brick shithouse (a shithouse where, one presumes, the water flushes in reverse). The pair have previously done the TCC in just over three minutes, which places them second and third on the all-time list, speed-wise. Nick has also brought two Aussie mates along to show us mellow-bellied Brits how it's done.

As we sit around a large table near Mission's front door, The Proprietor strolls over to tell us the rules: 'There are very few rules,' he says, his chin almost reaching the tabletop. 'It's all going to come in one go. Once we shout "go" you can touch the food. You can't until then. To complete the challenge you have to finish absolutely everything on your tray. You don't have to swallow everything by the time I say "stop". But if you can get it all in your mouth, we'll stop your time. There are basically no other rules. Though you are going to be abused quite heavily.'

Then he brings out a sick-bucket and places it in the centre of the table. It is joined at the feast by our host/abuser for the next ten minutes, Holly. And her megaphone.

With some drinks ordered ('No beer … trust me,' warns The Proprietor), the trays of meat are brought out and the countdown begins.

And then … before I could finish cutting my burger tenderly into bitesize pieces (a bum tactic, for what it's worth), we're a minute in. And although I'm here to report on proceedings, it's difficult to focus on what else is happening around the table. This is because The Proprietor is shouting bad words in my ear and telling his staff to force feed me.

Across the table, Andrew is contentedly sat with 16 Chili Cheese Fries sticking out of his mouth, the tentacles of a potato squid slowly being sucked to death. As some of us take a third bite, his burger is already being attacked. Nick is even further along.

As the abuse levels grow, it's becoming very clear that I'm not going to win. As Andrew stuffs his last few fries into his mouth with his paw, I start on my second item. Ten minutes may not be long enough. But at least Jack, Aussie #2, is struggling too.

Nick and Andrew both finish in under four minutes and are soon comparing tactics. Tactics which looked from the other side of the table a lot like putting as much food in your mouth as is possible and then shoving more in with your fingers.

Luke, Aussie #3, finishes in just over seven respectable minutes. By this point I'm gasping for air. Jack and I endure a further two minutes of sustained personal abuse before hobbling over the line like a pair of fat Derek Redmonds. Except instead of a dad carrying me over the line I have The Proprietor cackling and pouring me a punishment whisky. We've failed. Nick has won. Andrew came a close second. No one, it must be said, needed the silver bucket. Now I just have to go and pay my bill.

THE TRIPLE CHILI CHALLENGERS

ANDREW MALPASS (previous best time 3.27)
Age: 35
From: County Durham, now London
Biggest meal eaten: I had like a kilo of steak in Spain. It was for two people. And I had a whole Chateaubriand on the same holiday. I also had an entire deep-pan 18-inch pizza to myself once.
How he prepared: When we did the TCC for the first time, my mate who did it with me (and failed) was texting me all these ridiculous plans to prepare. I thought, I'm not going to bother planning it, I'm going to eat the burger first and see what I fancy. The next thing was to eat the hot dog without the bun. And then eat the bun.
Eating inspiration: None, really. I've always just really loved food. Apart from girls, it's probably what I think about most.
Time taken: 3.41

JACK KONDER
Age: 23
From: Melbourne
Biggest thing previously eaten: Honestly, I couldn't tell you.
How have you prepared for tonight: I haven't done anything. I had lunch. A peanut-butter sandwich, my friend.
Eating heroes: That bloke off *Man v. Food*. He inspired us to do this.
Time taken: DID NOT FINISH

LUKE SKEWES
Age: 24
From: Melbourne
Biggest thing previously eaten: I once had a massive, massive rump steak. I'm not sure the weight of it – it was at home – we cooked it up. It was a lot easier than this.
Eating hero: These guys [he means Nick and Andrew].
Time taken: 7.23 ['It was tough, I thought I was doing really well with my hot dog, but the chips just undid me.']

NICK SACK
Age: 27
Previous best time: 3.36
From: South of Melbourne
Biggest thing ever eaten: I've done some big steaks, but I did the Red Dog challenge at the Red Dog Saloon, too. That was big, but the biggest was probably a 1.5 kilo steak in Florence.
How did you prepare for tonight: We went out last night, which wasn't the best preparation. For lunch I had chicken and vegetables. I thought I'd better go healthy.
Eating hero: I have watched *Man v. Food* a fair bit, so probably Adam Richman.
Time taken: 3.39

WILL DEAN

Age: 29

From: Manchester

Biggest thing ever eaten: I didn't actually manage to eat much of it, but the ridiculous maple-based feast served by mad Canuck genius Martin Picard as his Quebec Sugar Shack on MEATliquor's tour of Montreal. It included a chicken leg stuffed with lobster, a table-sized offal pie, an omelette covered in brains and lardons and crispy gizzards. I've not been the same since.

How did you prepare for tonight: I had Macaroni and Cheese from the terrible canteen in my office. A mistake, in hindsight.

Eating hero: I've always respected the big-hitters: your Five-Bellies, your Bristows, your Bloodvessels. Sadly, as my showing here suggests, I'd be unable to compete with them in a Cool Hand Luke-style egg-eating contest. So let's just say Gregg Wallace.

Time taken: DID NOT FINISH [*Ed: 'Boo-hoo-hoo'*]

TRIPLE CHILI CHALLENGE

1 2.47 SITENG StanMa
2 3.27 ANDREW Malpis
3 3.36 Nick "The nut" Sack
4 3.36 MENUCO
5 3.43 Graham @ALWAYSSIPPIN'
6 4.01 MAX EURO-BOOB
7 4.22 Justin Time (what a guy)
8 4.29 STEVE KID
9 5.02 MOUCH & POPPY ♥
10 5.04 JOHN V

✝

20 HOURS IN MEATliquor

By Stefan Chomka

IT'S 6 a.m. on Saturday morning outside a grubby-looking building beneath a carpark near Oxford Circus Tube station. A smell of burgers hangs in the air, intermingled with the strong scent of cheap perfume. To the left of the building is a strip club, just closed for the evening, its staff filing wearily out of a side door. To the right is MEATliquor, which, a few hours earlier, had been rammed but now sits eerily silent in the early London gloom. The morning kitchen staff are entering through the same door from which the night staff and the strip-club girls are leaving.

Kitchen staff get to work straight away because the day's ingredients have come in the night before, between 11 p.m. and the small hours – by 4 a.m. the kitchen is bursting with food. Quickly they set about their jobs, which routinely include chopping mountains of pickles, onions, jalapeños and lettuce, slicing burger buns and preparing chicken wings and burger patties. It's a job that, for some, will remain a constant throughout the day, with half the kitchen continually prepping in order to keep up with demand. And demand is high. In an average week customers chomp their way through 1,250 Cheeseburgers, 1,200 Dead Hippies, 2,500 of its other burgers and a further 1,325 of mains, including Phili Cheesesteaks and Chili Dogs. They will eat over 3,800 portions of fries – enough to stretch over two miles if laid out end to end – and 1,045 portions of Bingo Wings. The restaurant takes delivery of around 750 kilos of meat each week. Customers get through two football pitches of kitchen roll to wipe meat juice and hot sauce from their fingers.

At 9 a.m. the booze is delivered. Over the course of a week more than 2,700 cans of beer are sold, along with 500 glasses of Grog – a powerful blend of light and dark rums that so punchy it's limited to only two per person. Some 3,000 other cocktails will also be guzzled. Given the name MEATliquor, the hard stuff was always going to be an integral part of the business, but its popularity took everybody off guard. 'We never expected to sell so many cocktails,' says barman Robb Collins, a man who sounds like he was named after a cocktail. The Henrietta Fizz (vodka shaken with muddled pear and strawberry, fresh lemon juice and fizz) is the most popular with the ladies, while the men predominantly opt for a St Lawrence (Bulleit rye whiskey with maple syrup and bitters).

MEATliquor doesn't take bookings. That means that at the start of the day's service front-of-house staff don't know whether they'll be serving 25 people or 1,000. Except the restaurant has been busy from the get-go, so the chances of them not getting bunions after a 12-hour shift is slim. The room has only 90 covers, with space for another 10 at the bar, but that doesn't stop it from serving over a thousand people on a busy day. 'The busiest night is Saturday,' says general manager Joe Bergin, the man who has the unenviable job of ensuring everything runs smoothly. 'From the minute we open it's full and it doesn't let up.' There are no split services and often no respite.

When the doors open at midday the wheels go into motion: they won't stop for at least another 14 hours. At 12 noon the room is empty, by five-past there are already four or five people sitting down. By 1 p.m. the room is full and buzzing. A lunchtime queue has formed and it begins to snake its way down the side of the building. It's been a common sight every Saturday in these parts since MEATliquor opened.

The queue is part of the experience at MEATliquor, and Sunday is there to make sure you 'enjoy' it. Sunday is MEATliquor's door supervisor, and he looks like he's been hewn out of wood. He goes down the queue and gives people a stamp, which is required to gain entry, meaning that if a latecomer of a group tries to jump the queue they will have to join the back. Everyone has to queue, although some don't believe this catch-all policy applies to them. 'We get people trying to blag their way up the queue all the time,' says Joe. 'A rich Arab once tried to bribe the doorman with £500.' His generosity was politely refused.

As a sweetener, staff hand out trays of food to those waiting in line, typically onion rings and pickles, and in the summer months jugs of iced tea. When customers finally make it over the threshold their seats are either promptly found or they are directed to the bar. Lingering customers are encouraged to vacate to the bar with the offer of free shots, then their seats are quickly filled. 'It's like human Tetris,' as Joe describes it.

You know that feeling when you go to the cinema and you come out blinking into the sunshine, as if woken from a deep sleep? You have a similar sensation when you leave MEATliquor after lunch. The restaurant is dark to the point of being cave-like. Back-lit stained-glass windows depicting scenes of debauchery and graffiti only add to the feeling of being in Dante's *Inferno* … or *Porky's*. And then there's the music, described by MEATliquor co-founder Scott Collins as a mix of hillbilly, swamp-rock and country, 'basically anything from Iron Maiden to Dolly Parton'. The clientele echoes this eclecticism. At one table a family with young children are tucking into burgers and coke floats while a group of Middle Eastern men are enthusiastically knocking back cans of Hobo beer at another. People in suits rub shoulders with unfathomably skinny men wearing spray-on jeans. Girls dressed to the nines mingle with others who have puffed their way from a nearby Fitness First. It's a microcosm of society where even vegetarians have been known to stray.

Between 3 and 6 p.m. still more trays of food navigate the room. By 6.30 the place is again at capacity and it will remain so until well past midnight, with the 15 front-of-house and 12-strong kitchen brigade offered no let up. There's been no time for any kind of pre-service pep-talk from Sophia Browne – the matriarchal figure known affectionately as Meat Madam – or to discuss tactics, but that doesn't bother the staff. In the corner, giggling can be heard from the photobooth, where customers have been known to get up to all sorts of shenanigans, says Joe. Can he share some examples? 'It's like Vegas. What happens in MEATliquor stays in MEATliquor,' is his guarded response.

By 9 p.m. the walls are reverberating to what sounds like Garth Brooks gargling acid. By 11.00 the place is more nightclub than restaurant. Its trademark aroma will be tattooed onto all its customers, who will wake up smelling like someone's rubbed them down with beef dripping and Buffalo sauce. At 1 a.m. the menu is reduced to just Dead Hippies and booze to give the staff a chance to wind down. 'By around 2.30 we'll want you to go,' says Joe. 'But we don't kick anyone out.'

That gives just enough time for the last tables to be cleared and the kitchen cleaned ready to start again. For some staff the night is still young and they will move on for a well-earned late-night drink; for others a visit next door might even be on the cards. It's all in a day's work for Britain's best burger joint.

I AM LOMO

A.K.A. A BRIEF HISTORY OF TAPAS

CURLED around the base of the rabbit warren of near-vertical alleyways that make up the Moorish Albaicín neighbourhood in Granada, Calle Elvira is seven hundred yards of tapas bars, all competing with each other to give you free food. Like all the best neighbourhoods, it's neither very poor nor very rich: whether it be from tourists smoking dodgy soapbar or from gypsies burning the finest Caramelo, the smell of hash permeates the air. Bankers walk shoulder-to-shoulder with anarchists; tourists chat easily with dope dealers.

You'll find Morrocan tea-shops sitting alongside Galician cider bars; snippets of Sevillanas wail out from the flamenco bars, doing battle with the gabba blaring from the squatted flats above them.

Señoras Who Lunch parade themselves at the zinc bar of an upmarket restaurant, while the punk bar next door plays host to dreadlocked stoners and coked-up hustlers. This particular bar also serves some of the best tapas I've had. This sandwich, a pork slider known locally as 'Lomo', is inspired by the one at this bar.

TAPAS IS STILL FREE BY LAW in Granada – but only with beer or wine, not with spirits. The origin of tapas (meaning 'cover') is shrouded in the mists of time (to say nothing of the fug of countless hangovers) and numerous legends have grown up around it: every toothless old man drinking himself to death in the darkness of an Andalucian bar seems to have his own version of the story. Here's some of the ones I can remember:

★ *King Felipe III was getting fed up with his peasants being pissed all day long so ordered that wine should only be served with a little plate of food.*

★ *One windy day King Alfonso XII stopped at a beach bar for a drink and a snack. Obviously a man with his priorities straight, the king covered his wine with the bread to stop the sand getting into his booze (because: fuck food). Upon finishing he ordered a second round of drinks, asking for them to be served with a 'tapa' again.*

★ *The Spanish army invented tapas to prevent hangovers.*

★ *King Alfonso X fell ill and could only eat small bites of food and a little red wine throughout the day. On recovering he declared that no bar in Spain was to serve wine unless it was served with a little bite to eat.*

★ *Lunch was for wimps: peasants didn't get their union-mandated one-hour lunch break back then. Instead they'd take frequent short breaks throughout the day when they'd eat small amounts of food and drink small amounts of wine. Of course, nowadays they take a three-hour lunch break and still spend the rest of the working day eating and drinking in the pub. This is why I love Spain.*

★ *In the days before insect-zappers, drinks were covered with a small plate of food to stop the fruit flies from getting at that sweet, sweet liquor.*

Peasants were spending all their money at the pub and then going home to beat their wives into mañana. Queen Isabella (maybe) decided she'd had enough and ordered that beer and wine (peasants couldn't afford spirits back then) be served covered with a small plate of food which would have to be consumed before the drink, thereby keeping them slightly more sober.

YP

WHAT YOU NEED

Serves 4

4 soft bread rolls
Mayonnaise
Tomato ketchup
½ red onion
320g pork loin cut into ½-inch slices
1 tbsp olive oil
1 tbsp thyme
1 clove garlic, smashed
A pinch each of sea salt and black pepper

WHAT YOU DO

Lay the slices of pork loin in the bottom of a deep dish. Add salt, pepper, thyme and the smashed garlic. Mix well, cover and refrigerate for 1–24 hours. Remove from the fridge 30 minutes before cooking.

Slice the bread rolls in half and smear mayo on one side and ketchup on the other. Heat a heavy-bottomed frying pan with a thin coating of oil. Don't let it smoke or it'll taste bitter.

Shake most of the excess oil and bits of garlic off the slices of pork loin and add them to the pan carefully – they'll spit oil. Cook them one or two at a time – don't overcrowd the pan or the temperature will drop and they'll get tough boiling in their own juices.

After a minute or so flip them: they should be slightly golden brown. After another minute, remove them from the pan and place on the bottom of the bread roll. Top with a few thin slices of red onion and cover with the top of the roll. Let sit for 2 minutes before eating so the heat from the Lomo has a chance to warm and soften the bread.

Drink: beer or wine. Not spirits.

ΧΩΡΙΑΤΙΚΗ ΣΑΛΑΤΑ

(GREEK SALAD)

S O MANY memories every time I make this dish …
The blistering heat of the midday sun … Hirsute,
sunburned German Fraus just barely contained by their
floss bikinis smuggling contraband food from the breakfast
buffet …

An octopus going round and round in a tumble dryer on
the beach …

A meal in itself.

A National Institution.

Every region, every taverna and every family in Greece has
their own version of this dish. Mine is inspired by one from
the mountains in the far north of Greece, near the Albanian
and Macedonian borders. My aunt used to make it on a
daily basis. It's a very different dish to what's served up to
blistering Brits at the beachside tourist traps.

GREEK FACTS

Kalamata olives are the big, purple juicy ones. They are very
meaty and succulent but are aggressive by nature and are
known to hunt in packs.

It's very important to have everything cold: this should
be a refreshing dish, full of crisp, crunchy vegetables.

You want large chunks – something to chew on.

Don't dress the salad ahead of time or it will go limp.

It's important not to mix the oil and vinegar into an
emulsified dressing – you want individual separate pools of
both EVOO and vinegar.

The feta is used in two ways: crumbled finely as a
component of the dressing, and also in larger chunks as
something you can really get your teeth into.

Try and get barrel-aged feta. It's worth spending the
extra when the cheese is the star of the show, like it is here.

YP

WHAT YOU NEED

Serves 4

4 large, ripe tomatoes, salted
1 cucumber
1 red pepper
1 red onion
150g Greek feta cheese
A dozen or so kalamata olives
3 tbsp EVOO (extra virgin olive oil)
1 tbsp red wine vinegar
1 tsp dried oregano
Black pepper to taste
Crusty white bread
Salt

WHAT YOU DO

Chop the tomato, red pepper and cucumber into bite-sized chunks. Slice the red onion thinly.

Place the tomatoes and cucumber in a strainer over a bowl and sprinkle with salt. Let them sit in the fridge for 20 minutes and the salt will draw out a lot of the excess water, concentrating the flavour of the tomatoes and keeping the cucumber crunchy.

Discard the water that drips off them or mix it with iced vodka for a refreshing shot.

When you're ready to serve, combine the tomatoes, cucumber, red pepper, red onion and olives in a bowl. Use your fingers to crumble half of the feta really finely into the bowl.

Add the oregano and a grind or two of black pepper and toss the ingredients together well so the feta and seasoning is evenly distributed.

Add the EVOO and the vinegar directly to the bowl together with a tablespoon of the marinade from the olives and toss the salad again, making sure everything has a good coating of oil, vinegar and feta cheese. Adjust to taste.

When plating up, scatter some larger, bite-sized chunks of feta on the top.

Serve with crusty white bread to mop up all the juice at the end.

Drink: ouzo.

THE DEAD HIPPIE

A HAIKU

By Yianni Papoutsis

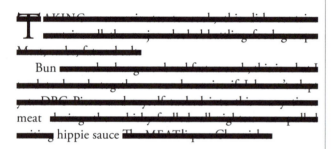

T̶AKING ▬▬▬▬▬▬▬▬▬▬▬▬▬▬▬▬
▬▬▬▬▬▬▬▬▬▬▬▬▬▬▬▬▬▬
M̶▬▬▬▬▬▬▬▬
Bun ▬▬▬▬▬▬▬▬▬▬▬▬▬▬
▬▬▬▬▬▬▬▬▬▬▬▬▬▬▬▬
▬DRG▬▬▬▬▬▬▬▬▬▬▬
meat ▬▬▬▬▬▬▬▬▬▬▬▬
▬▬ hippie sauce ▬MEAT▬▬▬▬▬

WHAT YOU NEED

2 slices ▬▬▬▬▬
250g of b▬▬
2 ▬▬
1 thick slice of melted cheese
S▬▬▬▬▬▬

WHAT YOU DO

▬▬▬▬▬▬▬▬▬▬▬▬▬▬▬▬▬
▬▬▬▬▬

▬▬▬▬▬▬▬▬▬▬▬▬▬▬▬▬▬
▬▬▬▬▬▬

▬▬▬▬▬▬▬▬▬▬▬▬▬▬▬▬▬
▬▬▬▬▬▬▬▬▬▬▬

▬▬▬▬ lettuce ▬▬▬▬▬▬▬▬▬▬▬,▬
75▬▬▬▬▬▬▬▬▬▬▬▬▬

▬▬▬▬▬▬▬▬▬▬▬▬▬▬▬▬▬
▬▬▬▬▬▬▬▬▬▬▬▬▬▬▬
▬▬▬▬▬

▬▬▬75▬▬▬▬▬▬▬▬▬▬▬▬▬
▬▬▬▬▬▬▬▬▬▬▬▬▬▬▬
▬▬▬ onion ▬▬▬▬▬▬▬▬▬▬
▬▬▬▬▬▬▬▬▬▬▬▬▬▬

▬▬▬▬▬▬▬▬▬▬▬▬▬▬▬▬▬
▬▬▬▬▬▬▬▬▬▬

▬▬▬▬▬▬▬▬▬▬▬▬▬▬▬▬▬
done.

▬▬▬▬▬▬▬

FULL ENGLISH MARTINI

Courtesy of Giles Looker

WHAT better way to start the day than with a full English, and the same goes for this; be it first thing in the morning or just before dinner, this drink does exactly what the Martini is meant to do – stimulate conversation, whet your appetite, but most of all gives you a good slug of alcohol with a delicious, slightly salty snack at the end. The Full English Martini was created for the opening of MEATliquor. Instead of an olive we used a pickled quail egg rolled in dried bacon, which we created by frying the bacon till burnt and then hydrating it with maltodextrin. To make this drink in the comfort of your own home you can get similar results by rolling the pickled quail egg in a bag of crushed up Frazzles.

WHAT YOU NEED

75ml gin
15ml dry vermouth
Quail eggs

FOR THE PICKLING MIX
300ml white wine vinegar
20 whole black peppercorns
20 juniper berries
2g salt
4 orange peels

FOR THE BACON POWDER
6 rashers of unsmoked bacon
1 pack of Frazzles crisps (crushed)
Maltodextrin
Oil for frying

WHAT YOU DO

Cook quail eggs on a rolling boil for 6–7 mins. Run under cold water for 5 mins. Peel eggs, discarding any whites that break revealing yolk.

Press juniper berries with the flat end of a knife to release the oils. Add with other pickling-mix ingredients to a saucepan and heat. As soon as the mixture begins to simmer, take off heat and pour over eggs in a sealable jar. Pickle for several weeks.

Cook off the bacon until almost burnt, then dry off the fat/oil using kitchen roll. Allow to cool.

Chop into very small pieces and add, with the pack of crushed Frazzles, to a blender. Blend and add maltodextrin, 2 spoons at a time, 6 spoons in total. You may need to add more if there is a high fat content in the bacon.

Roll quail eggs in the bacon powder.

Fill a mixing glass with cubed ice. Pour the gin and vermouth over the ice and stir (you should be looking to dilute 25ml water into the drink).

Strain into a pre-chilled cocktail glass and serve as soon as possible with an egg on the side of the glass (NOT IN THE DRINK).

DRINK in 60 seconds.

MEMPHIS STEAMER

Courtesy of Giles Looker

THE Memphis Steamer was created out of many trips to New Orleans spent drinking in after-hours rhythm-and-blues bars on Frenchmen Street. The real drinking in New Orleans is found out of the tourist reach in a small area known locally as the 'Barmuda Triangle' which comprises three bars that you can never seem to leave, across the road from each other. They don't boast the best drinks, music or food, but they are bars for drinking and talking no matter what time of day or night it is.

For the Memphis Steamer use Southern Comfort Reserve, which is 40% abv and is blended from a base of six-year-old straight bourbon and is often only available to UK residents in Duty Free.

This is a Sazerac-style drink, although fruitier as it calls for crème de cerise (cherry liqueur), which works well with the fruit flavours in the Southern Comfort Reserve. Add a few dashes of absinthe and it perfectly balances.

This sums up the city of New Orleans. What could go wrong when drinking in this fantastic city?

WHAT YOU NEED

50ml Southern Comfort Reserve
15ml crème de cerise
3 dashes of absinthe

GARNISH
Lemon twist and Luxardo maraschino cherry

WHAT YOU DO

Place all ingredients into a stirring glass over cubed ice; stir until chilled and diluted. Strain into a cocktail glass and express a lemon twist over the drink and place in a coupette.

And DRINK.

Order another.

FALLEN ANGELITA

A TREATISE ON RIMMING

Courtesy of Giles Looker

THE Margarita. (The best drink in the world!) This drink is a mystical beast, and a great one at that. No one really knows how it came about and no one should really get their knickers in a twist about it. The story I like the best is that Margaret 'Margarita' Sames from Dallas, famous for throwing crazy parties in Acapulco in the 1940s, came up with it. Essentially, it is a tequila Side Car, substituting tequila for brandy, lime juice for lemon, and salt rim for sugar.

A great variation on the Margarita is from Tommy's restaurant in San Fransico, by Julio Bermejo. Instead of using orange liqueur he uses organic agave nectar. Julio also assisted us in arranging to pick up 50 cases of Arette Tequila, fresh lime juice and Cointreau and take it to the Burning Man Festival where we made Margaritas for the whole festival – eight days straight. (Day 5: severe heartburn.)

Here is a recipe served at all the MEAT restaurants incorporating both a classic Margarita and a Tommy's, and adding just a touch of honey for a floral flavour.

WHAT YOU NEED

45ml El Jimador (or any good 100% agave blanco tequila)
10ml agave syrup
10ml triple sec
25ml lime juice
5ml honey

GARNISH
Tajin* and a lime wedge

WHAT YOU DO

Place all ingredients into a Boston shaker and shake, strain over cubed ice in a highball glass which has been rimmed,† garnish and DRINK.

* A lime chilli salt from Mexico.
† Take your glass and a wedge of lime, press the lime flesh onto the rim of the glass all the way round the outside. Then take the tajin or salt (for Margaritas) and pour onto the outside of the glass. Do this over a plate. Use the same lime again to wipe inside the glass just to make sure no tajin/salt is inside. Half-rimming is a hallmark of civilisation.

:::::::::::::::::::::::::::::::::::
:::::::::::::::::::::::::::::::::::
SCOTT
:::::::::::::::::::::::::::::::::::
:::::::::::::::::::::::::::::::::::

1. RICH IN PARADISE (GOING BACK
   TO MY ROOTS) - FPI PROJECT
2. KNOW HOW - YOUNG MC
3. O.P.P. - NAUGHTY BY NATURE
4. WHITE LINES (DON'T DO IT) -
   GRANDMASTER FLASH
5. PACIFIC STATE - 808 STATE
6. STRINGS OF LIFE -
   RHYTHIM IS RHYTHIM
7. ANTHEM - N JOI
8. THE REAL WILD HOUSE -
   RUAL ORELLANA
9. YOU'RE GONNA MISS ME -
   TURNTABLE ORCHESTRA
10. BREAK 4 LOVE - RAZE
11. PROMISED LAND - JOE SMOOTH
12. PLAYING WITH KNIVES
    (QUADRANT MIX) - BIZARRE INC
13. CHIME - ORBITAL

THE LESSON OF THE MARKET

THE MEATliquor CHRONICLES
PART SEVEN

444 words (sister of the Beast)

TRUTH is gleefully dealt with at the market. The cow is disembowelled, flayed, bled and dripping from a nostril on the head which sits apart from its carcass, staring bleakly.

Its tongue dangles free, ready to be cut.

From the leather cavern of the hole where a churning bowel used to hang, a smell of arse with blood and sawdust pours out into the rain. The butcher snips and chops, laughing heartily. He shouts a joke about a vagina while a man yells a penis back. They cut and gouge and curl back waxy slabs of a creature that lived without knowing that it would die.

It died and here is the truth of it. A man killed it and now like carrion two more fat men chop it apart. This is what they do, it makes them happy to do it, and keeps their conscience clear.

Tomorrow all the chunks will go to a halfway house of Truth. These stinking slabs would be a police matter if anyone saw them in the road. The Truth is now a police matter. So at the halfway house it will be cut into smaller pieces until none looks like part of a living thing.

Then to another house, the last before Truth is rendered dead. When no trace of it remains, the pieces will be ready to enter the parallel world. Resting on foam and wrapped in glossy plastic, as tight as a drum, the joke about the vagina bounces clean off. The joke has vanished and the stench has gone. Little Dominic, already ever so clever at the computer, can complain that he wanted something else for tea; some deep-fried lung-casing, gizzard and vein, formed into the shape of a drumstick.

Back in the market something waits in darkness.

Lights burn high above it while music plays through a haze of flame-grilling. The MEAT daddy has brought a temple with flames next to the market, symbol that no Truth is lost in the flavour of his meat. The distance between cow and joke and flame and hunger can be walked in half a minute. Jokes can be heard from the flames, and a faint breeze of arse, soot and fat can waft to the jokers.

But revellers eating beside the flames look down into the market, searching for the reason why a temple of meat should sit there. Because the cows are now memories long gone. Hooves and heads and tongues and Truth are things of a richer past. Money came to the market and replaced them. Now Chinese plastic, promises and lies haunt the gutters where blood once ran.

That's why the temple is there.

DBC

'Every moving thing that is alive shall be food for you.'
And they all go with Chili Fries

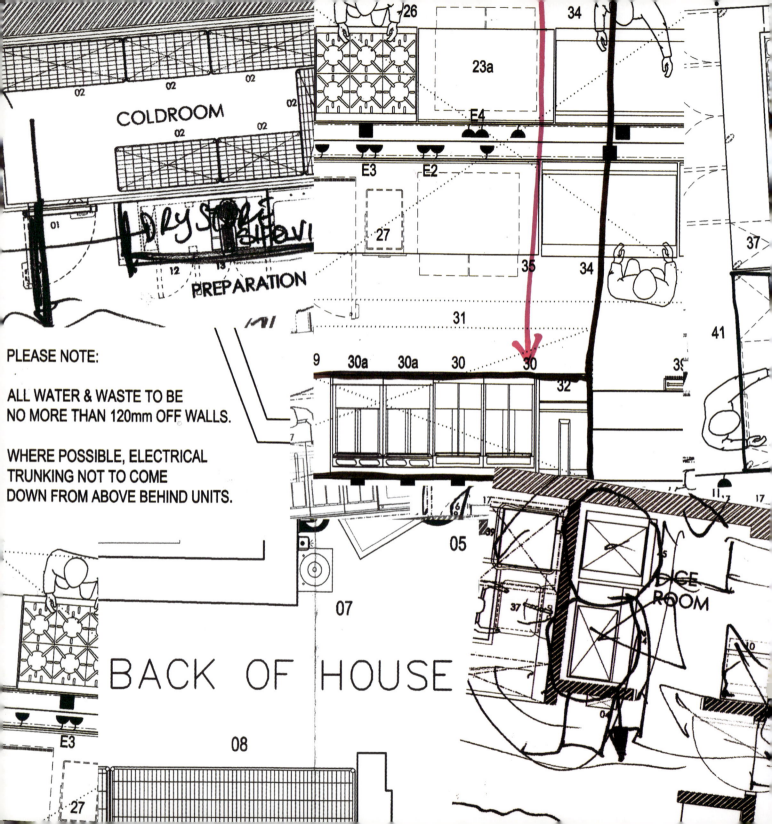

COLDROOM

DRY STORE SHELVI

PREPARATION

PLEASE NOTE:

ALL WATER & WASTE TO BE
NO MORE THAN 120mm OFF WALLS.

WHERE POSSIBLE, ELECTRICAL
TRUNKING NOT TO COME
DOWN FROM ABOVE BEHIND UNITS.

BACK OF HOUSE

ICE ROOM

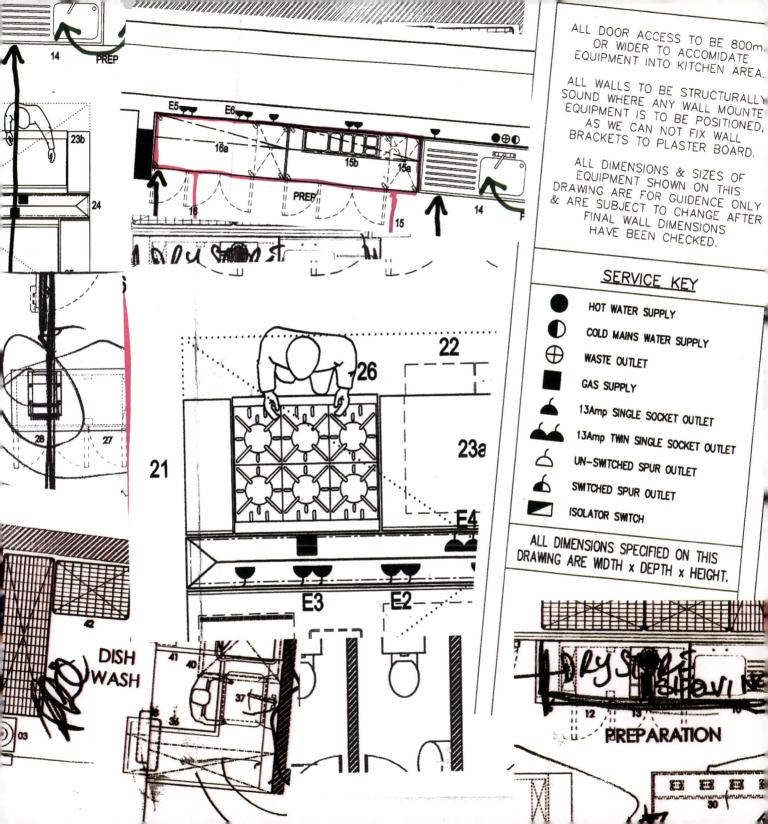

14 PREP

E5 E6

23b

16a

24

15b 15a

PREP

16 15

14

22

26

23a

21

E4

28 27

E3 E2

DISH
WASH

42

41 40

37

38

03

ALL DOOR ACCESS TO BE 800m
OR WIDER TO ACCOMIDATE
EQUIPMENT INTO KITCHEN AREA.

ALL WALLS TO BE STRUCTURALLY
SOUND WHERE ANY WALL MOUNTE
EQUIPMENT IS TO BE POSITIONED,
AS WE CAN NOT FIX WALL
BRACKETS TO PLASTER BOARD.

ALL DIMENSIONS & SIZES OF
EQUIPMENT SHOWN ON THIS
DRAWING ARE FOR GUIDENCE ONLY
& ARE SUBJECT TO CHANGE AFTER
FINAL WALL DIMENSIONS
HAVE BEEN CHECKED.

SERVICE KEY

● HOT WATER SUPPLY

◖ COLD MAINS WATER SUPPLY

⊕ WASTE OUTLET

■ GAS SUPPLY

13Amp SINGLE SOCKET OUTLET

13Amp TWIN SINGLE SOCKET OUTLET

UN-SWITCHED SPUR OUTLET

SWITCHED SPUR OUTLET

ISOLATOR SWITCH

ALL DIMENSIONS SPECIFIED ON THIS
DRAWING ARE WIDTH x DEPTH x HEIGHT.

DRY STORE SHELVING

12 13

PREPARATION

30

MEAT MARKET

ICE CREAM

FOO

MEAT ▶▶ MARKET

CHICKS

74.

KIWI HOBBIT
maul him and show him the stars. Will do anything. Any/Things in this no. Scandinavians should apply. Knowledge of Ursa Major essential small but perfectly formed. requires a Great @pubhobbit

DON'T WANT TO QUEUE @MEATliquor?

SHAKES

CORN DOGS

A STAPLE of State fairs and snack stands in the States, it wasn't until 2012 when we visited Portland, Oregon, that I tried one that wasn't unspeakably foul. Scott had found this little place way out in the suburbs, and we both pedalled through the rain on rented bikes to eat their corn dogs the following day.

They inspired the following recipe …

YP

WHAT YOU NEED

200g fine cornmeal
200g plain flour plus extra for rolling sausages
8g baking powder
250ml whole milk
3 eggs
150g caster sugar
8g salt
Sausages – we favour a New Orleans-style Andouille,
*   but you can use whatever you like*
Vegetable oil

WHAT YOU DO

Mix the cornmeal, plain flour, salt and baking powder in a mixing bowl.

In a separate bowl whisk the eggs with the sugar and the milk.

Whisk ingredients from both bowls into a smooth batter. Roll each sausage in flour then dip in the batter. You may have to repeat this to get a good coating depending on what skins your sausages have.

Deep fry in vegetable oil in small batches at 165 °C until they are golden brown.

Serve with whole grain mustard and honey, either mixed or individually.

Drink: a boxcar of Hobo.

NAME: Dan a.k.a. Plon
DRINK: vodka
MEMORY: lost, along with laptop

THE BLACK PALACE

INSPIRED by an American burger chain's technique of steaming burgers over onions, but dedicated to those late, drunken nights in London when the air is redolent with the irresistible smell of fried onions from the purveyors of meats of questionable origin.

This is messy.

YP

WHAT YOU NEED

160g freshly minced chuck steak
1 small onion, thinly sliced
Vegetable oil
2 slices American-style cheese
1 burger bun
French's mustard
3 slices pickle
Salt and pepper

WHAT YOU DO

Heat 1 tbsp vegetable oil in a heavy, preferably cast-iron, pan over a medium heat.

Add the sliced onions.

Separate the meat into 2, equal-sized balls.

With a stiff spatula or burger slice, press each ball down on top of the onions until they form 2 equal-sized disks, about an inch larger than the diameter of the bun you're using.

Salt and pepper the top side of the patties generously then cover them with the remaining onions.

When the onions have browned and a golden crust has formed on the meat, flip the patties, and press down slightly into the onions.

Add a slice of cheese to the top of each patty.

Cut the bun and add to the pan, toasting it slightly and steaming it with onion juice.

When the patties are cooked to your liking, remove the bottom of the bun from the pan and spread a thin layer of mustard over the grilled side and top with pickle slices.

Remove the first patty from the pan, and add to the base.

Top with some of the fried onion.

Add the second patty with the bun top to your burger. Let rest for a couple of minutes for the flavours to amalgamate.

Eat.

Serve with: napkins. Lots of them.

TIGHT BROWN

MAPLE BOURBON SHAKE

Courtesy of Giles Looker

HARD shakes are one of the most difficult drinks to balance correctly. We bloody love them and I think this is the ultimate hard shake.

One bit of advice: follow the recipe. The biggest mistake in a hard shake is over-pouring the booze. This recipe calls for 25ml of bourbon. If you over-pour it becomes too dominant and you lose all the flavours. This is the same with most drinks; you can always add more but you can never take away. So as much as it pains me to say, this drink is not a great drink to get drunk on, but it's a bloody tasty beverage and one I always look forward to.

Maple and bourbon go together like drum and bass and we first started serving them at MEATmarket. When making this drink at home make sure you use a good-quality ice cream.

WHAT YOU NEED

25ml Bulleit bourbon
15ml maple syrup
1½ balls of vanilla ice cream
80ml whole milk

WHAT YOU DO

Place all ingredients into a blender and blend until a good, thick consistency.

Pour into a highball glass. DRINK.

THAT FOREIGN MUCK

THE GOSPEL OF FOREIGN IGNORANCE

THE MEATliquor CHRONICLES
PART EIGHT

555 words (valet of the Beast)

IT CAN happen that a revelation arises at once in a variety of peoples not in contact with each other. The extent to which an idea is true can be judged by the number and scale of these random instances.

The MEATdaddy, the marshal and the intoxicator no sooner realised the scale of their quest and duty than they immediately wondered which others might have suffered a similar blow of Truth. Who else was casting out false prophets and moneylenders from their temples? Which other seers had felt a rod of unusual Quality upon them?

In order to understand that rod we must first apprehend all divinity. How can it be, for instance, that a hundred gods are worshipped on the basis that each alone is the true god and all others are false? How can this especially be so when many of those gods dictate the same terms and promise the same salvation?

With due respect to each of these and to their worshippers, it can only be explained like this: we must imagine a sun comprising all divinity and Truth. From the storms at its gaseous heart it makes all heat, all life and therefore all love, sending beams of these to all beneath it. That sun is the single God, the single Truth.

Imagine now that it sits nestled in a colander. Its qualities are unchanged, it remains the single Truth; but its shine is split into identical beams, a hundred of them, and where one falls closer than another to a worshipper, although he can see other beams on the horizon, he correctly sees that, for being closer, his beam is brighter and hotter than all the others around.

So upon that single rod he attaches all Truth. He spreads that Truth to others not so close as him, and in the number of people nearer to him than to another beam, he has a congregation.

What they worship as divine and absolute is not all sunlight, but a rod of sunlight.

In explaining that a hundred beams of identical light can have a hundred interpretations we only need note that each interpreter is different, and that his biases and fears come to bear on his interpretation. It's because of this that we forever fight to the death over divinity; we fight without seeing that battles are waged over bias, not light itself. Like all who receive a sunbeam, our trio, as unexpected seers, were forced to imagine how shamans in other beams were interpreting their Truths. Perhaps they would have a better Truth; perhaps between us and them we could arrive at a greater interpretation of Truth than either alone; in any event all were brethren united under light.

With this understood, feeling curious, hopeful and cautious, the legion set off to the west, spreading gospel along the way. Perhaps those foreign beams would be stronger, brighter than theirs. Perhaps those foreign prophets would understand more, and as a result be further along the path of their mission.

In the end we could only admit that whatever difference existed between beams, all were by nature equal and could be neither better nor worse than each other.

This noble mindset accompanied the Crusade, till the first foreign shaman spoke.

'Yo, Limeys.'

And the legion suspected that his beam was comparative shit.

DBC

MEATBALLS WIDDA RED SAUCE

IMMORTALISED in popular culture, this dish has played a starring role in both *Goodfellas*, where Paulie and Vinnie make Meatballs and Sauce in prison, and also in *The Godfather* in the scene in which Clemenza tutors Michael Corleone in the finer points of sauce.

I first tried this Italian-American dish in a small, family-run trattoria in a strip mall on a solo mission to New Jersey; it blew me away. I put this recipe together over a number of years, evolving it until it approximates what I *remember* the original tasting like. In my opinion the best meatballs really are made with beef, pork and veal mince: veal for texture, pork for fat and beef for depth of flavour.

The Red Sauce should be rich and unctuous and is an integral part of the dish rather than a separate topping: the Meatballs are browned very slightly first for a bit of caramelisation, then finished off by simmering them very gently in the Red Sauce, imbuing them both with each other's flavours and tying the dish together.

The resting is very important here, both for the overall flavour and the texture: serving them immediately after cooking will produce leathery, chewy Meatballs.

YP

WHAT YOU NEED

Serves 6

600g beef chuck mince
200g pork mince
200g veal mince
2 eggs
3 cloves garlic, finely chopped
1 small onion, finely chopped
50g dried breadcrumbs
25g grated parmesan cheese
½ tsp each of salt and black pepper
A pinch of white pepper
A small handful of finely chopped fresh basil
A small handful of finely chopped fresh flat-leaf parsley
A pinch of fennel seeds
A splash of white wine
A splash of milk

FOR THE RED SAUCE
25g pork mince
140g tin of double-concentrate tomato paste
1 medium onion, finely chopped
5 large garlic cloves, finely minced
3 x 400g cans of whole plum tomatoes
Salt and pepper
Sugar to taste

WHAT YOU DO

In a large bowl combine the meats, mixing well with your hands. Add eggs, one at a time, mixing each one in well. Add the remaining dry ingredients and mix well. Add a small splash each of milk and white wine and mix through. Let the mix sit for 20 minutes for the flavours to amalgamate. Have a glass of wine maybe?

With your hands, roll the mixture into balls about the size of a golf ball, adding either a splash of milk or a handful of breadcrumbs if the mix is too dry or wet for easy balling.

Heat a good slug of olive oil in a deep, heavy-bottomed saucepan until a drop of water sizzles in the pan, then fry the meatballs in batches, turning constantly until *just* browned. Remove from the pan, shaking off any excess oil and set aside on paper towels to drain.

Using the oil from the meatballs, fry the pork mince in a little olive oil until just browned, then remove from the pan and set aside in a bowl.

Fry the tomato paste in a little olive oil for a few seconds. Then add the onions and fry gently until they just start to brown. Add the garlic last so it doesn't burn and fry gently until the colour just starts to turn. Add the fried pork mince back into the pan, mix well then add a good splash of white wine, deglazing the pan a bit as you do. Add the tinned tomatoes and break them up well in the pan with a spoon. Add salt and pepper to taste, and a pinch of sugar if the tomatoes are acidic to balance out the flavour.

Simmer over a very low heat, stirring regularly for about 30 minutes or until the sauce is smooth and lump-free.

Add the fried meatballs to the just-simmering tomato sauce and continue cooking for another 5 minutes or until the meatballs are *just* cooked. Take the pan off the heat, cover and leave to rest for at least 20 minutes to let the meatballs relax.

Serve over al dente spaghetti topped by a dusting of Parmesan or smothered with melted mozzarella or provolone in a meatball sub.

Drink: Valpolicella or a Barolo.

THE CASINO CLUB

DEAD of night.
A motorway.
Any motorway.

The Road is far from glamorous: bleary-eyed from too many hours staring down the centre line, mind fugged by all kinds of white-line fever, knuckles bulging and stomach knotted, the distant lights of tonight's sanctuary beckon.

The car's pretty much parking itself by this point.

A man takes a credit card in exchange for a key card.

Base instincts take over.

Piss. Done.

Smoke. Done.

Drink. Done.

Now eat.

It's well past the witching hour. The restaurants are all shut up tight.

Any cook with any talent has left work and is currently getting messed up on their drug of choice at the closest/cheapest bar/brothel.

Every nerve cries out for sustenance: stimulants will only get you so far in this life, boy.

One choice remains: that stained and dog-eared rectangle of card buried at the back of the faux-leatherette 'Welcome' (translation: 'Fuck you') pack.

Why even bother reading it? You know it better than your own address by this point: a cynical selection of nukeable nastiness that can be prepared by even the most exploited night-shift worker.

Thai Curry.

Bolognese (always with a really inappropriate pasta).

Caesar. Fucking. Salad.

And there, tucked away at the bottom, a glimmer of hope in a sea of culinary despair.

The last resort of the hungry insomniac:

The Club Sandwich.

It promises everything a peripatetic inebriate might require in a late-night meal:

Toasted bread.

Roasted bird.

Crisp lettuce.

Juicy tomatoes.

Hellman's mayo.

Crisps.

Easy.

Trembling fingers stab at the buttons on the phone.

Half-understood insults are traded with a disgusted operator.

Somehow an order is made.

Add a bucket of ice and …

Somehow this has cost forty quid.

Whisky is drunk.

Weed is smoked.

News is watched.

Ablutions are performed.

The anticipation reaches a zenith.

More whisky is drunk.

More weed is smoked.

Clean enough already: more weed is smoked.

A knock.

The door opens.

Ganja smoke billows out into the face of some poor bastard who's pulled the night shift.

Eyes are averted.

Signatures are taken.

Grubby notes change hands furtively in exchange for discretion.

Somehow this has now cost fifty quid.

But …

Food.

A cloche is raised.

A crest is fallen.

How can anybody get something so simple so fantastically wrong?

Soggy, cold, half-toasted bread; anaemic tomatoes; wilted lettuce; limp bacon; rancid mayonnaise; flaccid poultry.

No sodding crisps.

How do they fuck this up?

Every. God-damned. Time.

Here's how not to.

YP

WHAT YOU NEED

3 slices white bread
Butter
Good mayonnaise
4 slices smoked back bacon, cooked crispy
1 small chicken breast
1 large tomato
I slice Swiss cheese
Iceberg lettuce
Salt
Ready salted crisps
1 whole dill pickle
Coleslaw (see p. 60)
Cocktail sticks
Avocado (optional)

WHAT YOU DO →

TOAST

BUTTER ADDS LUBRICATION TO TOAST

CHICKEN PULLED APART INTO MANAGEABLE CHUNKS

MAYO STICKS THE CHICKEN TO THE LETTUCE

LETTUCE, TOMATO, SALT

MAYO BINDS THE TOMATO TO THE TOAST AND STOPS IT GETTING SODDEN

TOAST

ONLY BUTTERED ON THE BOTTOM, MAYO ADDS LUBRICATION TO THE TOP

BACON MUST BE CRISPY, NOT LEATHERY

CHEESE HOLDS THE BACON IN PLACE

BUTTER FOR MORE LUBRICATION

TOAST

C O C K T A I L   S T I C K

TURBO PRAWN COCKTAIL

Hosted by Torgren Torgrensson

THE only quadruped to have graced the early Icelandic sagas, the noble prawn – or 'Plon', in Icelandic – is still revered for its alluring scent, creamy flesh and haunting cry on a winter's night. Known in Iceland as the 'crackly girl', the prawn has been known to lure many a brave seafaring man to his death. Arctic Circle prawns can reach the size of young horses, able to challenge large invertebrates and even shipping because their skeleton is worn outside the body. Many a submarine returns from the Northern Passage covered with dents from these feisty tricksters of the sea, which can only be disarmed by immersion in boiling water. After treatment in this way they finally become docile and ready to be undressed. Which is more than can be said of Mrs Torgrensson.

Here then is a recipe for docile crackly girl.

WHAT YOU NEED

Serves 2

10 large prawns – uncooked, shell-on
Peppercorns
2 unwaxed lemons cut into wedges
A pinch of celery salt
Crushed ice
Parsley

FOR THE SAUCE
4 tbsp tomato ketchup
1 tsp vodka
1tsp grated fresh horseradish
A dash of Worcestershire sauce
A dash of sherry
A dash of Tabasco
A squeeze of lemon juice
A pinch of cracked black pepper

WHAT YOU DO

Mix all the ingredients for the sauce together then set aside in the fridge for at least 30 minutes for the flavours to amalgamate.

Boil half a pot of water with a few peppercorns and a couple of slices of lemon. Add the prawns, shell-on, for a couple of minutes until they're just pink.

Remove the prawns from the water and place straight into a large bowl full of water and ice. Leave them for a few minutes to cool before shelling them.

Serve over crushed ice garnished with parsley, lemon wedges and celery salt.

Drink: chilled white wine or ice-cold beer.

✝

THE SOUTHERN HEMISPHERE NEW YORK

Hosted by Torgren Torgrensson

ONE interesting feature of this place is the almost total lack of English spoken, except for the words 'New' and 'York', which are often spoken twice among this disoriented race. Despite having recourse to a vast English-speaking continent, almost as big as Australia, a great many souls have come to this one rocky islet in the sea, where like termites they build great towers and live on top of one another. After some investigation I discovered why: it seems they all at one time fled persecution in their native lands, but arrived to find the barbarity even more dire than at home. Now, like flightless gulls, they perch and teeter on the easternmost edge of the continent, looking fondly back on the lands they judged too harshly. Indeed, they are slowly being rescued as a busy traffic of ships will attest, bound in the direction of Europe. More recently someone had the foresight to erect a statue at sea to serve as a warning for those arriving. It depicts a woman uglier than my wife's mother, with ice-picks through her head, brandishing a large flame. No traveller can miss its implications.

My advice: sit down and stay at home.

1 White Castle — Home of the slider 24/7 drive-thru.
2 Gray's Papaya — Late night dogs & papaya juice (good for the digestion).
3 Le Veau d'Or — 60-year-old classic French institution.
4 Abboccato — Hotel restaurant serving impeccable Italian cuisine.
5 Sake Bar Hagi — Late-night boozing and snacking.
6 White Castle — Home of the slider.
7 Keens Steakhouse — An institution. Steak & seafood.
8 Izakaya Ten — Late night boozing and snacking.
9 240 9th Ave
10 Trailer Park Lounge — Off-the-wall party bar. Great vibe.
11 The Jane Hotel — Cool bar apparently.
12 The Standard, High Line — The place to stay.
13 Rocky's — Pizzaaaaaa!
14 The Donut Pub — Fried donuts 24/7.
15 Dave's Army Navy Store — My go-to shop for all my workwear.
16 Bleecker Street Pizza — One of the classic NY slice joints.
17 Pearl Oyster Bar — Lobster rolls, fried oysters & more ...
18 Joe's Pizza — The archetypal neighbourhood slice bar.
19 Do Hwa — Owned by Quentin Tarantino.
20 Una Pizza Napoletana — Neapolitan pizza.
21 Veselka — Ukrainian, open 24/7.
22 International Bar — The Dive.
23 Milano's Bar — An old-school neighbourhood drinking den.
24 Balthazar — The Daddy of all brasseries.
25 Torrisi Italian Specialties — Insanely good Italian sandwiches & tasting menu.
26 Ray's Pizza — Great late-night slice stop.
27 Double Down Saloon — Get double drunk.
28 Sigmund's — Brunch, pretzels.
29 Meatball Shop — Does exactly what it says on the tin.
30 Mission Chinese Food
31 Umbertos Clam House — Mob food at its best.
32 Wo Hop — 70 yrs old & still open 24/7.
33 Adrienne's Pizzabar
34 Grimaldi's — One of the last coal-fire pizza ovens left.
35 egg — Williamsburg breakfast joint.
36 Fette Sau — BBQ in Brooklyn.
37 Beer Boutique
38 Pies 'n' Thighs — Fried chicken.
39 Duff's Brooklyn — Metal bar. Loud.
40 Di Fara Pizza — Neapolitan-style pizza.
41 Jay & Lloyd's Kosher Deli — Meat on rye. 'Nuff said.
42 Randazzo's — Classic Brooklyn Italian fare.
43 Nathan's Famous — Coney Island hot-dogs. One for nostalgia buffs.

KALIMOTXO

Courtesy of Giles Looker

THERE are times when we must all face the confined quarters and inadequate sustenance afforded by cattle class. When the trolley trundles around and you're faced with minuscule cans of mixers and tepid beer, there is a drink which provides refreshment, alcohol and caffeine and can be concocted using just two ingredients from the on-board bar.

The Kalimotxo.

Although the name is Basque, it's known by a multitude of other names all across Spain. A mix of red wine, cola and ice, it is a drink that is very much more than the sum of its parts.

YP

WHAT YOU NEED

1 small bottle of airplane red wine
1 regular (or 2 small) cans of cola – anything will do
Ice

WHAT YOU DO

Charm cabin attendant into providing you with 2 drinks.

Mix red wine and cola 50/50 over ice. DRINK.

Serve with: whatever you're given.

✟

THE WORST THING THAT EVER HAPPENED TO ME

By Will Dean

FIRST, some previous humiliations: at an interschool sports gala I once tripped over my own legs attempting a triple jump and fell face-first into the sandpit, 10 metres in front of every attractive, sporty girl in the Metropolitan Borough of Oldham.* On the eve of my eighteenth birthday I was turned away from the door of Manchester's second-worst nightclub, despite having a ticket, for being two hours too young to get in.† I have been called a 'snotty little Tory cunt' on the Internet by fans of an indie band,‡ despite being neither a Conservative nor small.§ Brother, I know humiliation.

All these moments were nothing compared to the events of the 6 March 2013 (evening) when a naive agreement had been put in place to drink with Yianni Papoutsis and Scott Collins in the worst bar in New York.

We'd spent the day trawling around some of New York City's best places to eat – Roberta's, Fette Sau, Momofuku Ssäm – like a load of pale, beer-gutted basking sharks. Basking sharks who, instead of plankton, eat a preposterous amount of pork. A stupid amount. More-than-a-thieving-abattoir-assistant-could-smuggle-into-a-bin-and-then-pick-up-after-work amount of pork. There was also some orange wine, at one stage. Frankly, I still don't know what orange wine is. It looked like IrnBru. But wasn't as nice as IrnBru. [*Ed: What is?*]

Anyway, this bar. It's called Hogs and Heifers and it's opposite the designer Diane von Fürstenberg's shop, and our hotel, The Standard. This is New York's Meatpacking district. Here, people do their best to look at you (well, me) with something approaching arched, withering pity. Even when

you're paying $11 for a bottle of Peroni. Great.

Hogs and Heifers' schtick is to play really loud good ol' boyish music for about 21 hours of the day. To the extent that you can hear 'Nine to Five' from about three blocks away. And you can smell the sleaze from eight. Obviously Scott and Yianni were drawn to it like moths to a turd-covered flame.

So, in we went.

With a vibe of union-organised punchups, Hogs and Heifers is not the place for a speccy loser whose idea of a hard drink is Carlsberg Export. It was certainly not the place to enter into rounds of Rolling Rock with Maker's Mark chaser with those two maniacs. I began to lose count after six. But I had already had at least three and a half glasses of orange wine.

I should have perhaps seen the warning signs when Hogs and Heifers' two bikini-wearing barmaids picked up a megaphone each with which to abuse their customers.

At first they were playing nicely, muting the songs clobbering out of the dusty PA system and drawling their own verses in the increasing silences that followed. An act that seemed rather impressive until you realise that it's the same 19 songs driving the Von Fürstenberg customers and the poor valet at The Standard Hotel apeshit throughout the day, and therefore not learning the lyrics to each song would have been more difficult than learning them.

The megaphones also serve as a wonderfully effective way to tell the leery weirdos brave enough to make a pass at the barmaids (I was surprised to find that I wasn't in the immediate company of any of them) to go and fuck themselves. That's what they said, these girls: 'Go and fuck yourself.'

Clearly, it was almost brilliant. But still terrible. The walls were covered in memorabilia from the local Teamsters and construction unions throughout the years.¶ Though anyone inquisitively sober enough to pay them anything beyond the scantest of attention was quickly told in no uncertain terms by a sixfootwide bouncer, 'This ain't a fucken museum, buddy.'

The toilets too were quite something for a city as anal as New York. An unspeakable pool covered the floor, the ceiling was decorated with wet toilet roll balls (of the comprehensive-school-toilet variety) and the sink … well, it seemed wise not to touch the taps, let's put it that way.

But our gang of Yianni, Scott, Giles and the other hacks who'd made it past bedtime stayed put. No Soho House for us. We stayed and we drank crap lager. And we followed the crap lager with shots of Maker's Mark. And we played pool. Not very well, but we played pool. Then there were more drinks. And then someone farted.[||] And then the terrifying barmaids remarked upon the fart.[**]

And then it happened.

When one of the bar girls saw the beginning (and continuation) of a wince on my face as the seventh shot of whiskey began to trickle down my throat, the obvious reaction was to grab the megaphone and point out the misdeeds of the English pussy over by the pool table.

Yeah, but she didn't do that, did she?

What she did instead, bless her cold, dead heart, was to simply stare with her vacant eyes at your correspondent until his pupils met hers. Once the two pairs were aligned, her beer-sticky hands rose to the sides of her eyes to recreate a gesture understood around every society in the world to mean 'What the fuck are you crying about you LITTLE FUCKING CRYBABY?' (Or just 'Boo-hoo', whatever.)

It was, with scant exaggeration, the worst thing that has ever happened to me. The most succinct and efficient three seconds of humiliation a Gorgon with a megaphone in a bikini top could possibly dole out. She got me. She got me good.

Now, that alone would have been enough to crush my ego. Alas, things were made worse by my companions in Hogs and Heifers proceeding to spend the rest of the evening (and the next five days travelling around New York City and Montreal) making the said-same 'boo-hoo' gesture in my direction every time I opened my mouth. Which was really funny. Ha ha ha. Ha.

Before long, waitresses were being bribed to spring a surprise boo-hoo on me as I asked for another drink. Virgin Atlantic flight crews were popping up with a blitzkrieg of boo-hoos just when I thought the worst was over. Thankfully, British Customs staff don't take kindly to offers of financial bribes from incoming passengers, so a boo-hoo was avoided as we returned to Britain.

But that was the only exception. Before I could tell my wife about all the special new friends I'd met on my trip, the Greek one started sending me picture messages from the entire staffs of MEATliquor and MEATmission boo-hooing the shit out of me. Then the customers. I'd become a meme. And then they forced me to write about the whole ordeal in this book to ensure my pain is recorded until the last 10 copies are pulped from the remainders section in the Harrow branch of The Works.

So, yeah, cheers for that.

---

* Last place, triple-jump competition – Oldham Schools Athletics Cup 1997–8.
† 42nd Street, off Deansgate (where 'home-grown Manc heads Chris, Mike and Damien entertain the world with an always changing mashup of classic and modern indie'). You would hate it.
‡ Little Man Tate, rubbish.
§ 5' 11" and a bit
¶ Moustaches. Thousands of them.
|| He knows who he is.
** It was Scott.

THE BOO-HOO

Courtesy of Giles Looker

I DEVISED the Boo-Hoo in Will's honour, as he is unable to drink bourbon in the conventional manner without welling up like a scolded child. But you need not be as unusually delicate as him to enjoy it. Be sure to make the ginger syrup in advance – it will keep for up to five days refrigerated.

WHAT YOU NEED

40ml Maker's Mark bourbon
20ml lemon juice
20ml fresh ginger syrup
10ml sugar syrup
Rolling Rock

GARNISH
3 lemon wheels
Fresh tears

WHAT YOU DO

For the fresh ginger syrup: pour 1l of water into a saucepan and bring to the boil. Add ⅔ cup of finely chopped ginger and 5 tbsp of sugar, and simmer for 30 mins, stirring occasionally. Pour through a fine sieve, pressing down on the ginger to extract all the liquid. Cool before use.

Place Maker's Mark, lemon juice, ginger syrup and sugar syrup into a cocktail shaker, add cubed ice and shake. Strain into a beer mug or a highball glass over cubed ice and top with Rolling Rock. Garnish and DRINK.

WHEN MEATliquor WENT STATESIDE

A COLLECTION OF VIGNETTES

By Stefan Chomka

PROLOGUE

THERE is a bottle of Japanese whisky – Yamazaki 12 year old, to be precise – suspended from the ceiling of a Montreal bar by a magnet. It's one of many bottles that hang like legs of jamon in a Spanish tapas joint, tantalisingly within reach yet simultaneously out of bounds for anyone except its owner. This particular one has the word 'meat' scrawled on it in black marker pen, as well as a signature and a rather poorly drawn sketch of a cock and balls, presumably so its owner Scott Collins will know it's his.

The bar, a late-night hangout for Montreal's insomniacs, is called Big in Japan, although whether it takes inspiration from the 1984 song of the same name by German synthpop group Alphaville is debatable. It's no 'Musik-Club', for starters, although bad knitwear, terrible haircuts and ill-fitting trousers are a common theme among its clientele – including ourselves. But if you want to go to a place where drinks hanging from the light fittings is its schtick (and who in their right mind doesn't?) then BJ, as it will henceforth be known, is the place to go down (to).

BJ displays your whisky bottle for a year, which it believes gives the drinker ample time to see it to the bottom. After that its effervescent yet diminutive owner André Nguyen presumably puts it back behind the bar or adds it to a giant vat of Yamazaki in which he bathes to keep his skin looking supple. We, on the other hand, are in Montreal for a mere 48 hours and only have a limited amount of time in which to drain it. Needless to say, given the amount of other booze on our agenda, we don't succeed.

So if you happen to find yourself in the Plateau Mont-Royal area of the city in the small hours, look for a seemingly unmarked red door covered in graffiti and a tiny plaque bearing a Japanese inscription. Inform the kindly bar lady therein that your name is Scott, point to the bottle with a cock on it, and with a bit of persuasion she'll probably stand you a glass of 'meat liquor'.

NEW YORK: NIGHT ONE

New York isn't a city, it's a swirling mass of temptation.

Once we've been spun around and spat out by the humourless all-American welcome that is homeland security – 'You dare to come into *our* country you English layabouts?' – heads thick with the effect of numerous glasses of champagne, Cyder Cars (see p. 92), espresso Martinis and God knows what else we got through on the flight over, the city is ours. We've blagged upper-class seats to New York courtesy of 'limousine in the sky' Virgin Atlantic via its excellent Heathrow lounge, although there wasn't much sitting involved, more loitering around the well-stocked bar. Vertical drinking at 35,000 feet: it gives a new meaning to the term 'bar-fly'.

Within an hour of leaving Newark we're encamped at the bar on the nineteenth floor of The Standard Hotel while girls in short gold dresses more provocative than wrong-un Kim Jong-un after a skinful serve us drinks. Outside the Statue of Liberty is flicking us the bird, the Hudson River as enticing as a three-way with Jedward.

It's then on to dinner at The Grill downstairs where the bartender produces every cocktail on the extensive menu. The group is thus: MEATliquor's Scott Collins and Yianni Papoutsis, Giles 'Good' Looker from booze consultants Soulshakers and a smattering of hapless journos – including myself and the *Independent*'s Will Dean, soon to become the 'Terry Waite' of the gathering. The aim of the jaunt is to seek inspiration for this fine book in your hands (can't you tell?) but in reality it's a thinly veiled excuse for us to cross the pond and consume as much, and as varied, food and hard booze as we can.

If you don't know MEATliquor then crawl out from the fried-chicken bargain bucket you've been hiding under. The punky burger 'empire' is run by Yianni, a small man of Irish and Greek descent (although his surname hides it well), who wears the tired, wild-eyed look of someone coming down from a four-day bender but who'll happily talk Kafka with you and argue over the difference between a palanquin and a sedan chair (after 20 minutes I'm still not sure there is one?) and Scott. Scott is a tall, bald and slightly menacing-looking fella thanks to his sleeve tattoos and thick gothic bracelet, whose tireless enthusiasm means his life is just one endless carousal. Scott – or Shot, as he should have been christened thanks to his propensity for calling impromptu rounds of shooters complete with a swirly finger motion for the bar staff – won't talk about Kafka, but he'll drink with you until you won't be able to pronounce it either.

Brains and brawn. Little and large. Ren and Stimpy. Call this odd couple what you will (mostly not to their faces), it's a formidable match made in meaty heaven. And they've come to the Big Apple to take a mighty bite out of it.

NEW YORK: NIGHT TWO

It's 2 a.m. on a Wednesday night in the Meatpacking District. We're in a notorious dive bar being shouted at through megaphones by two bikini-clad (female) bartenders for not parting quickly enough with our dollar bills. Dusty Harleys and moose heads hang on the walls, and there's a photo of some bikers with their faces scratched out as if they may be no longer with us. A huge hulk of a man sits on a stool on the far side of the room, possibly guarding the toilet, which doesn't have a lock and which makes that one in *Trainspotting* look like the Palace of Versailles.

Outside it's threatening to snow. It's the end of a very long day.

Let's rewind 12 hours. Over this time we've attempted to consume steamed pork buns, duck wings, a whole pork butt and dozen oysters for lunch at Momofuku Ssäm Bar, followed by enough fried chicken to make Tooting High Street blush at Momofuku Noodle Bar for lunch number

two of the day. We've also visited smoke pit Fette Sau in Williamsburg for a meat fest that took in Berkshire shoulder and belly, loin chops, sausages and sauerkraut, as well as some formidable Key Lime Pie, so we now all smell like we've got 40-a-day cigar habits. What we didn't eat we had bagged up for us and we trawled the streets of Manhattan looking for someone suitably needy on which to unload our bounty, although my line of 'Excuse me, sir, fancy some butt?' didn't reap the happy response I'd expected (except once, but that's another story). We finished our feasting off at Roberta's in Brooklyn for a late pizza supper that involved far too much Parmesan and not enough pepperoni for all our likings.

Now, full of carbs, riding the meat sweats and giddy on orange wine that tasted of cider, we're being hollered at by New York's finest bartending duo, who are now up on the bar top dancing and shouting obscenities at anyone within earshot and making the occasional 'boo-hoo' gesture at one of our party (see Terry Waite's piece). All we can do is drink more overpriced beer, neck Maker's Mark (thanks Shot) and pray this place closes to save one of us from suggesting to leave.

It doesn't. We stay for another couple of hours until we've all had one too many experiences with Versailles. Then, with the bar girls' voices still ringing in our ears (as they chase us with a megaphone) we call it a night.

MONTREAL: NIGHT ONE

Joe Beef. It's the reason we upped sticks from the comfort of New York's capacious bosom and took a collection of cancelled and extremely late planes (thanks, the weather and Air Canada) to Montreal. It's all because the restaurant's cookbook of sorts *The Art of Living According to Joe Beef* (they should have called it *Meet Joe Beef*) has lured Scott and Yianni into Mountie territory like a pair of groupies to a Beyoncé gig. If the book's this good, goes their train of thought, what's the place itself going to be like?

The answer, to paraphrase a respected restaurant critic, is 'fucking good'. We kick off with a starter of Horse Tartare followed by Donkey Mortadella that kicks like a mule, and then oysters. Lobster Spaghetti is artery-cloggingly thick and rich in all the right ways, then comes Rabbit Stew and what must be the world's best jacket potatoes that come slathered with bacon and cheese. The *pièce de résistance* is a horse steak topped with a frankfurter amid a foie gras sauce, so fine you could name a Grand National runner after it and people wouldn't take offence (see pp. 176–7 for the recipe). No one told the pastry chef the 1970s were over with pudding coming in the form of a booze-soaked halved pineapple smothered in whipped cream and glacé cherries. We ate some before Scott wore the rest as a mask. We all agreed it was a huge improvement.

Later, we grab a taxi and lament that we're not JB regulars while being forced to listen to Scott's phoney French accent as he talks to an increasingly incensed Creole taxi driver with a hatred for music – and also now Scott. We decide that we love Montreal: the feeling isn't mutual.

MONTREAL: NIGHT TWO

We thought our long-distance journey to eat Canada's best meal was over once we hit Joe Beef, but as our private car winds its way through the dark, deserted country roads of Quebec we're not so sure anymore.

We've been travelling for over an hour and a half, supping furtively on bottles of sake smuggled aboard when our driver wasn't looking – the spoils from an ill-advised yet utterly wonderful pre-dinner dinner at sushi restaurant Park that Scott and I partook in – and none of us has the faintest idea where we are. All we have is a poorly drawn map and the confident endorsement from our hotel's concierge that 'there is no damn way you've managed to get a table there' ringing in our ears. And then suddenly it's in front of us, a cross between Porky's and the house from the Blair Witch Project, and every bit as inviting yet sinister: Au Pied de Cochon Sugar Shack.

Sugar shacks, or 'cabanes à sucre' as they are known, are common in Quebec. They were primarily places where maple syrup is produced until one bright spark decided to serve food and created a whole new genre of restaurant. De Cochon is a bit different, however.

First of all you can't get a reservation. Seats for the entire maple syrup season sell out in a matter of hours, generating a booking stampede Justin Bieber wouldn't 'beliebe'. And when you sit down at the table that you can't possibly have got in the first place you're treated to the weirdest meal of your life.

DINNER AT AU PIED DE COCHON SUGAR SHACK

A Play in Three Acts

Act One

We are seated at a long table that we share with a group of ten young-ish Canadians. The noise in the room is not dissimilar to the House of Commons in full voice, thanks to the poor acoustics of the wooden structure. The atmosphere is that of a frat party, so also not too dissimilar to the House of Commons.
WAITRESS: 'We've been open five years and the pastry chefs are unhappy that people don't have enough room for dessert, so we're going to serve it to you first.'
She brings over a towering starter platter of popcorn, candy floss, marshmallow cookies that look like Tunnock's teacakes, canelés, almond croissants and ice cream cones. Everything is made with, and often coated with, maple syrup, which means it looks like our waitress had a collision with a tin of Ronseal on the way to our table. To finish there are shot glasses of Jack Daniel's to knock back, happily to cut through the sweetness, so we think. Except this is maple-laced JD so it's as refreshing as downing a pint of black treacle.
YIANNI: [*shooting back the syrupy JD with a wince*] 'I'm pretty full already, I hope there's not much more …'
Our waitress clears our starters. A procession of courses then follows. But this is no tasting menu of small plates, oh no, but giant-sized portions. We are served:

1 Tourtière du Shack – a whole pie filled with no less than one pig's trotter, shredded pork shank, bacon, pecan nuts, foie gras, calf's brain, veal sweetbreads and half a wheel of Laracam cheese

6 pieces of Salmon Jerky – smoked salmon fillet vac-sealed in maple syrup for two months

1 whole hock of maple-glazed ham and a pile of boiled potatoes

1 duck-and-lobster stuffed chicken with green beans

6 barbecued duck legs

The table is quiet as we desperately try to find ways of disguising how little we have eaten.
WAITRESS: 'Can I get you guys a beer?'
ALL: 'Yes please. What have you got?'
WAITRESS: 'We have a nice maple-flavoured one.'
ALL: 'Actually, we'll stick with wine' [*the only thing on the menu not made with maple syrup*].
Lights fade, as does our enthusiasm for life.

Act Two

WAITRESS: 'Have you finished your mains?' [*Her eyes scan the table, still heaving with half-eaten food.*]
ALL: 'Err, yes.'
WAITRESS: 'Then I'll bring you your dessert.'
SCOTT: 'But we've already had …' [*The waitress has already gone.*]

Act Three

Dessert arrives in the form of Maple Yogurt Jello, a thick slice of blancmange with cubes of maple jelly set inside; Maple Taffy that comes on sticks to be dipped in vanilla ice cream, and a huge wedge of Angel Food Cake topped with a layer of bright white icing as thick as the King James Bible and just as palatable. Scott, meanwhile, dressed in a black and white stripy top has donned Yianni's hat and in a maple-induced stupor is pretending to be French.
WAITRESS: 'Can I get you anything else?'
SCOTT: 'Non, merci.'

The performance ends. Suddenly there is a 50-strong queue of people, paper bags of uneaten food in hand, waiting to pay their $59 and high-tail it back to civilisation, the sweet, sickly smell of maple syrup clinging to their bodies like Willy Wonka's onesie. Our table is the only one left in the room. The lights go up.

TEN LEARNINGS FROM MONTREAL/NEW YORK

★ *A bar on an airplane is a very good idea.*
★ *Pies can be divisive.*
★ *Ping-pong is NOT the same as table tennis.*
★ *There is never a hungry homeless person in New York when you want one.*
★ *You can crack walnuts with your head – eventually.*
★ *Canadian publicans do not believe in purchasing locks for toilet doors … bringing a whole new meaning to the term 'public toilet'.*
★ *Maple syrup and smoked salmon do not good bedfellows make (unless you like fishy Haribo).*
★ *Bagels can be divisive.*
★ *Pea lollipops will never catch on.*
★ *Will Dean drinks like a little girl.*

EPILOGUE

Martin Picard, the owner of Au Pied de Cochon Sugar Shack, is a big bear of a man. In fact he's exactly the kind of man you'd imagine would be behind a sugar shack on steroids.

With his unkempt hair and beard and lumberjack shirt he holds court, drink in hand, over the evening's proceedings from the bar, seemingly oblivious to everything that is happening around him. While all the other diners make for the door, we invite ourselves over for a chat. Picard obliges by cracking open a fresh bottle of Bushmills, which is instantaneously drained and shared among us. It's as if he's been waiting all night for someone to have a drink with.

Accompanied by a second bottle of Bushmills, Picard takes us to see his maple sap dehydrator, the beating heart of his business. It's lying dormant for the night and one suspects his mood is intrinsically linked to its actions. Turn it on and you can bet the maple syrup coursing through its pipes makes Picard's blood pump just that little bit faster too.

It's impossible to pigeon-hole Au Pied De Cochon, apart from to say it is outside of restaurant norms. From serving dessert first to putting squirrel sushi on the menu (there isn't a recipe for that in this book) it is about as conventional, and PC, as a papal lap dancing-club. In the UK Picard would most probably be sectioned and the restaurant declared unsafe based on the glycaemic index alone. Thankfully the Canadians see things differently. If you get the chance to not get a table, do take it.

Picard, who has been drinking steadily throughout the night, suddenly says he's up early in the morning, hence why he has been taking it easy (??), and we recognise our hint to leave. As we head back to our car, where our frustrated driver has been waiting for us for the best part of four hours – Scott: 'We'll be about an hour and a half' – there is a palpable pang of regret among us that we'll probably never eat at this brilliant-but-batty place again. Either that or we're experiencing the early symptoms of type 2 diabetes; none of us are entirely sure.

An hour and a bit away there's a bottle of 'meat liquor' with our (Scott's) name on it. And a drawing of a cock.

THE END …
… EXCEPT FOR ONE QUESTION:

'If you had to have sex with a building, which one would it be?'

Scott posed this particular conundrum to numerous waiting staff across Quebec, Montreal, Manhattan and beyond, while the rest of us shifted uncomfortably in our seats. Sometimes it was met with confusion, occasionally disbelief and, in one case, utter revulsion. But in general it yielded a surprisingly considered response. And the most popular answer from our American and Canadian cousins? La Sagrada Família. What a cultured bunch of fuckers.

THE MONEYSHOT

A.K.A. THE ALE FLIP

Courtesy of Jack McGarry and Sean Muldoon,
The Dead Rabbit, New York City
Hosted by Will Dean

FLIPS started out life in the colonial taverns of America and were made with a flip dog (loggerhead)* and it generally consisted of ale, rum, some type of sweetener and spices. However, the New World flip – born in the middle of the nineteenth century – was somewhat different. It was anchored by either hard liquor or liqueurs, some sweetener, almost always cream and a full egg. The Ale Flip bridges these two styles.

If you're lucky enough to make it to The Dead Rabbit Grocery and Grog you'll see this listed on their bulging menu as the Ale Flip. And you will be lucky because it's probably the best bar we've ever been to. Even Giles was crying green tears when he saw Jack and Sean's upstairs Parlor Bar.

Jack McGarry and Sean Muldoon are two of the world's finest bartenders. They turned the bar at the Merchant Hotel in Belfast into one of the planet's finest before legging it from Northern Ireland to plan The Dead Rabbit. It opened, after two years, in late 2012.

If you've studied New York immigrant history (or watched *Gangs of New York*), you'll know that the Dead Rabbits were one of the toughest Irish gangs in mid-nineteenth-century New York. Muldoon and McGarry's bar might be located deep in the centre of capitalist thuggery that is twenty-first-century downtown Manhattan,† but it takes its cue from the fighting Irish who came to New York

two hundred years earlier. Downstairs is a fine, fine Irish pub. Upstairs is the Parlor, where mixed drinks from the time of the Dead Rabbits are served with a bloody precision. (The Ale Flip comes from Jerry Thomas's *Bartender's Guide* of 1862.)

Now, Yianni is obviously a man who isn't unfamiliar with the concept of having a frothy liquid splashed all over his face. Unfortunately, Jack is a man unused to spilling drinks. After generously showing us around and fixing us an Automobile (from Tim Daly's *Bartenders' Encyclopedia*, 1903), Papoutsis ordered an Ale Flip. McGarry deftly mixed the ingredients and began to lift the finished drink over the bar.

What happened next can almost certainly be attributed to the fact that McGarry had to stretch so far over the bar to reach the small Greek man [*Ed: I've fucking told you, pal*]. As he did, the stub of the flip glass caught the Dead Rabbits' box of salts and fruits and was slingshotted through the dark Manhattan air and into Papoutsis's face. Eggy froth. In his face. Boo-hoo-hoo.

As amusing as his companions found this, Jack – who probably does this once a decade – was mortified.

But to preserve the memory, we asked him if we could use the Moneyshot – as it shall henceforth be known – in this book. He very kindly said yes. So you ought to be so kind as to go and make it. Or get on a plane, ask for 30 Water Street and order one yourself. Trust us.

WHAT YOU NEED AND WHAT YOU DO

Add these into a shaker:

60ml Powers Irish whiskey
30ml spiced syrup‡
7.5ml Suze¶
2 dashes Dead Rabbit Orinoco Bitters§
1 egg

Add one chunk of ice and dry shake.
Add ice and shake again.

Add 120ml Dead Rabbit cask-conditioned ale‖ into
the shaker.

Fine-strain into a pre-chilled flip glass and finish with
freshly grated nutmeg.

* It's a piece of iron about two feet long, with one end thicker
  than the other. One end was heated in the fire and thrust
  into the mug of grog, heating it all up and causing a froth
  to run over the sides of the mug. Also used to heat punches
  and toddies. Nowadays, considered a fire risk.

† The Dead Rabbit's location near Wall Street can make it
  somewhere for the *Bonfire of the Vanities* crowd to hit on
  a weeknight. Fuck those guys. We turned up at 2 a.m. on a
  Saturday while everyone else was in Brooklyn. Do it like this.

‡ You might have to make your own syrup for this – boil water
  and sugar together, chuck in some cinnamon, cloves and
  cardamom while it's boiling. Let it sit for 20 mins, then strain it.

¶ French bitters flavoured with the roots of the gentian plant.

§ When he was researching the drinks menu at the Dead Rabbit,
  Sean found an old ad in George Winter's *Nineteenth
  Century Cocktail Creations* (1884) for something called
  Orinoco Bitters, which claimed to be 'superior to any
  Angostura in the world'. The address given for its makers
  was 32 Water Street – next door to The Dead Rabbit. Thus,
  Orinoco Bitters became the house bitters of The Dead
  Rabbit. They're made for them now in Scotland by Adam
  Elmegirab (bokersbitters.co.uk) but you can probably get

away with using Angostura. Just don't tell Sean.

‖ Unless you work in downtown Manhattan you might have to
  improvise a bit here. The Dead Rabbit's own ale is a dark
  English mild made for them by the Sixpoint Brewery in
  Redhook, Brooklyn. Try a bottle of something like
  Harviestoun's Old Engine Oil instead.

SALT COD, CREAM AND POTATO PIE

Courtesy of Margot Henderson
Hosted by Stefan Chomka

LIFE is full of disappointments. Like discovering that you're adopted and your real parents are Nazi war criminals or chewing through the latest Dan Brown novel only to find that the conclusion is every bit as woeful as the beginning. Yet these are mere inconveniences compared with the soul-crushing feeling brought on by being served an alleged pie.

We've all been there. That moment when you discover the pie you've ordered in a pub or restaurant, one that you've pictured in your mind – thick, golden-brown shortcrust pastry stuffed with bubbling goodness – turns out not to be a pie at all. But rather a stew. With a limp puff-pastry top. In a brown oval dish. It's ersatz and it's the embodiment of evil.

We're not talking shepherd's or cottage varieties (which everyone knows aren't real pies anyway) but those crimes against cuisine, those lid-topped hotpots masquerading as the real deal. You should be able to slice a pie. Pick it up with your hands. Build an ornamental wall with them. An alleged pie offers none of these options: you may as well have ordered the soup.

Margot Henderson knows which way her crust is buttered, as the recipe for her splendid salt-cod, cream and potato creation demonstrates. Yes, it contains potatoes but they aren't used as a lid, oh no. There is nothing alleged about this pie. But still don't try to use it for masonry work.

WHAT YOU NEED

500g puff pastry
250g salt cod
1kg of waxy potatoes, Desirée are good, peeled
4 cloves garlic, peeled
2 onions, peeled
A bundle of herbs (thyme, bay leaves, parsley sprigs) tied
1 lemon
3 bay leaves
20ml olive oil
40ml double cream
½ bunch flat parsley
6 ripe tomatoes

WHAT YOU DO

Soak the cod for approximately 24 hours, changing the water every now and again. The thicker the cod the more soaking is needed to desalt properly. Keep in the fridge while soaking or in a cold spot.

In a pot, cover the cod in fresh water, add the bundle of herbs and ½ a lemon. Bring up to a boil and simmer for 15 mins. Strain and leave to cool. Once cool de-bone and leave the flesh to the side. Peel potatoes and leave whole in water.

Roll out the pastry and line a 12-in. cake tin. Refrigerate overnight.

Preheat oven to 180 °C.

In a heavy-bottomed pan heat the olive oil, add the onions, garlic and bay leaves, turn the heat down and cook gently until soft. Season with a little sea salt and black pepper.

Slice the potatoes on a mouli, about 2mm thick, being careful of your fingers. Add to the pot with the onions and garlic, simmer and stir gently, let them all get to know each other.

Chop the parsley and add.

In your pastry case, put down a layer of potato and onions.

Cover moderately with the poached salt cod, another layer of potatoes and salt cod, finishing with potatoes. Add sliced tomatoes to one layer if you fancy.

Roll out the rest of your pastry and make a lid for your pie. Using a sharp knife make a whole and carefully pour in the cream. Then brush the top with egg wash.

Bake in the oven for approximately an hour and a half. Serve with a radicchio salad and sherry vinaigrette.

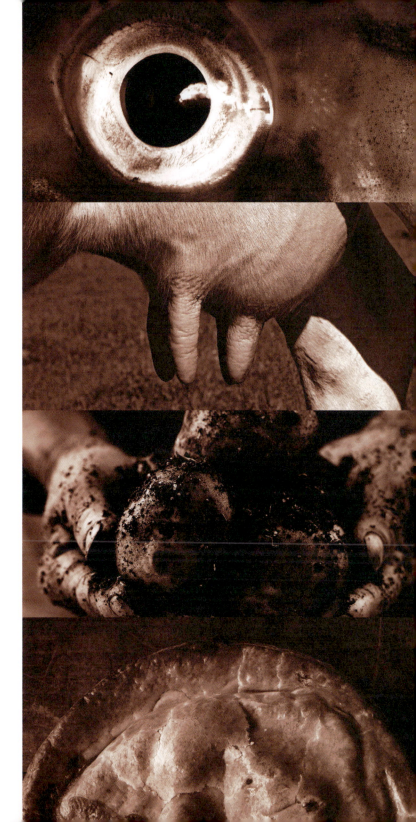

TOURNEDOS DE CHEVAL, FOIE AND FRANKFURTERS

Courtesy of Joe Beef, Montreal
Hosted by Torgren Torgrensson

THE horse is among the fastest of quadrupeds, and this alone accounts for its superb taste. Whereas a cow's meat will languish and rest fallow in a meadow, growing disinterested in life-giving nutrients, a horse's tissue is flying at full stretch, pumped full of adrenaline, which is the single most life-giving nutrient. If you doubt it, see what they use to revive the dead next to an ambulance.

As with all things in nature, those we must ingest the most to retain our powers are the ones which taste the best to us. And so it is with horse. This simple equation cannot be avoided even by science. As we say in Iceland, the horse is the most noble creature which can be eaten, and this is because its body is powered purely by male chromosomes; thus women are the least involved in it, compared to other foods. If you doubt this, look at who cooks your next horse – it is a man. And man, being the primogenitor with the most equipment, is the most capable of delivering that finite percentage of truly life-giving nutrients.

This is in marked contrast with puffin, which is almost solely endowed with opposite chromosomes, making it a cowardly and fickle bird, and very bad to taste.

My wife is calling me now to fix the whale-dryer.

Here is the finest recipe for horse.

Because putting a sausage on it is the culinary equivalent of 'the penis with shades' picture.

Note that the sausage takes 2 days. You will need a sausage stuffer for this recipe. And a cold-smoker. Meat thermometer highly recommended.

Makes 15 6-inch sausages. More than needed for dish, but no one ever complained about extra franks.

WHAT YOU NEED

Serves 4

4 350g horse fillet steaks
4 slices streaky bacon
1 foot of butcher's string
A pinch of steak spice

FOR THE FRANKFURTERS
1.3kg lean beef
900g pork back fat
70g salt
1g pink salt
670g crushed ice
70g milk powder
1½ tsp dry mustard
1½ tsp paprika
1½ tsp ground coriander seeds
½ tsp white pepper
25g chopped garlic
Medium-size pork casings
Maple-wood chips for cold-smoker

FOR THE FOIE CREAM
1 shallot, sliced thinly
1 sprig of thyme
2 tbsp Dijon mustard
100g foie gras
500ml of cream

Salt and pepper to taste
1 tbsp unsalted butter
Lemon juice

FOR THE RED WINE SAUCE
30g sliced shallots
½ small beetroot, peeled and thickly sliced
250ml dry red table wine
1 tbsp cheap-ass balsamic vinegar
1 bay leaf
250ml quality beef stock
1½ tbsp unsalted butter
Salt
½ tsp black pepper

WHAT YOU DO

For the frankfurters: cut all of the meat and fat into 1½-inch cubes. In a big bowl mix in the salt, pink salt, milk powder, garlic and spices. Let sit in the fridge overnight to marinate.

The second day: grind all of the meat (using the 'medium' attachment) in a grinder. Add the crushed ice. Place the meat in the bowl of a stand-mixer and mix with the paddle attachment at high speed until the meat and the fat are emulsified, about 10–15 minutes. It's very important to keep the meat chilled at all times, so while you're setting up the stuffer, transfer the meat to the fridge. When you're ready, stick in the meat thermometer … if you're under 15 °C you're all set. If not, continue to chill.

Pipe the meat into the pork casings, linking them so they are 6–7 inches long, depending on how you like your sausage. Cold-smoke them for 1½ hours and let them sit overnight in the fridge.

Put a large pot of water on medium heat and poach the sausages in simmering water until they reach 60 °C in the centre. Immediately dunk in ice water to cool and set aside.

Onto the horse: wrap a slice of bacon around each horse steak, tying it with a string. Season with steak spice. Cook the steaks medium rare or till they reach 48–50 °C in the centre. Set aside to rest, about 5 minutes.

For the foie cream: sweat the shallot and the thyme with the butter, add mustard and cook for about 2 minutes. When translucent, add the foie gras and the cream and cook at medium-high heat for 10 minutes or until the cream is reduced by a third. Season with salt, pepper and lemon juice. Buzz the cream with a hand-blender.

For the red wine sauce: in a small saucepan, mix together the shallots, beetroot, wine, balsamic vinegar and bay leaf. Bring to the boil over a high heat and reduce by half. Add the stock and continue to boil until reduced by half. Whisk in the butter and season generously with salt and pepper.

Place 1 horse steak per plate with 30ml of red wine sauce and 30ml of foie cream. Serve with 2–3 franks on the side.

ACCIDENTAL LIMOUSINE

Courtesy of Giles Looker

ON A return trip from Montreal to New York City, loaded on maple syrup and Japanese whisky from the previous night, we get to Arrivals and search for the name board of the taxi driver Scott said he had booked. We see the guy and follow him out of the airport. He walks us to our car; it's a long way through the car park. We seem to walk for ages; my bag feels heavier. We're hoping that each 4x4 we pass is ours. As we come to the end of the grey cold lot our hearts flag, then there it is – the longest, blackest car I have ever seen. No one knows why or how we ended up in this car but we didn't ask any questions. Our driver opened the door for us and we got in, laughed and helped ourselves to the free cheap-arse whisky it had on offer. This was our ride into New York City.

It was the Accidental Limo.

And here is the drink in its honour.

WHAT YOU NEED

60ml Yamazaki 12 yr
12.5ml grade 1 maple syrup
12.5ml sugar syrup
25ml fresh lemon juice
15ml egg white

GARNISH
Glacé cherry

WHAT YOU DO

Place the first 5 ingredients into a cocktail shaker and shake over cubed ice.

Strain into a rocks glass over cubed ice.

Garnish and DRINK. Try not to spill it going round corners.

A MISSION TO THE ORIENT

THE GOSPEL OF HELLHOUND

THE MEATliquor CHRONICLES
PART NINE

888 words (nearest bus stop to the Beast)

THERE are religious overtones to these chronicles because religion is human and we have licence to attach it to the things we find divine. But art imitates life imitating art, and at this point in the odyssey our real-life MEAT daddy finds a holy building to fill with dark exhilarations.

So it's time for a theology.

Long before Christianity arose, the legend of a hellish black dog took hold in many places at once; a dog with burning red eyes, supernatural strength, ghostly powers and deadly jaws who often hung around cemeteries. For the ancient Greeks he was Cerberus, charged with guarding the entrance to hell. Throughout England the Hellhound had many names and is still common folklore up and down the land; in Wales he's even seen as a benign force, though anyone who looks him in the eye is said to be sure to die. In Mexico he haunts country tracks preying on solitary travellers, and in Cataluña he's an emissary of the devil, lame in one leg. In Scandinavia he attaches himself to particular churches, protecting them from the dark one; in early Britain and Scandinavia a black dog was often buried in the corner of a churchyard for protection. So Hellhounds are among the most enduring supernatural manifestations, and are still seen around the world. The most recent sightings, in Connecticut, Kentucky, Louisiana, Ohio and Vilseck, Germany, were around cemeteries.

But why do they prowl through this book?

Because their symbolism leads to a question for we who identify with the spirit behind these chronicles; and that question is the heart of our theology. We reach it like this:

on Sunday 20 June 1937 on the third floor of 508 Park Avenue in Dallas, Texas, the Mississippi Delta bluesman Robert Leroy Johnson recorded 'Hellhound on My Trail'. It was the first song he recorded that day, and was the first single to be released from the session. A legendary song from a mystical musician we know little about. But what is known is remarkable, and ties you and us and him to an idea that paves a way to our question.

As a youngster Robert Johnson was known to be an appalling guitar player; credible witnesses attest to a complete lack of talent. Then, when he finally left the neighbourhood of his youth – some say to search for his natural father – he happened upon guitar legend Isaiah 'Ike' Zinnerman. Ike was known for having learned to play the guitar supernaturally, by hanging out in graveyards at midnight. He'd made a pact with the devil.

Zinnerman took young Johnson to play in graveyards. Legend says that one midnight Johnson met a large black man at a crossroads near Dockery Plantation, Mississippi, who tuned his guitar for him, and played a few numbers before handing it back. Blues folk across the region knew that the man was the devil; Johnson had sold his soul in return for mastery of the blues that made him famous.

It would all sound like bullshit if Johnson hadn't soon returned home with a miraculous grasp of blues guitar. Eric Clapton now calls him 'the most important blues singer that ever lived'. *Rolling Stone* ranks him among the top five guitarists of all time.

Johnson was 26 when he recorded 'Hellhound'. At 27 he was dead.

Nobody knows for sure where he's buried. Three markers exist in Mississippi which may or may not be his grave.

For the purpose of our question, the symmetry we want to draw from the man's life is that he had a burning desire, and had – or felt he had – nothing to quench it with. He made – or thought he made – a pact with the devil to let him rampage through the desire; then felt the devil's hound ravening after him to pay the price. He sang about the hound on his trail, expressing with that song what many consider to be the peak of his gift. Then he paid his toll and was gone.

Now let's isolate the feeling he must have had, the compelling urge to drink and keep moving, and apply it to us, to yourself. Look at us now. We weren't sucked into MEAT and liquor and blues for its family atmosphere. We don't prop up a bar because we're thirsty. We go to run. We go to confess and escape. From what? Our own Hellhounds – and we run just as fast and drink just as hard whether we made a bad pact or didn't make a pact at all. Hellhounds. Oblivion. Did Johnson run from them or to them?

And do we run from or to them?

Or are we the Hellhounds, pulling others into some pact? Lord knows we have burning red eyes and a foul odour some Saturday nights.

At the heart of all our parties, then, at the core of why we think waking up on a bar-room floor is cool, lies a theology with a mystery as in all good religions: what propels us there? What pact are we being chased for?

Do we run from or to it?

And if we can identify and ritualise that running, can its energy be harnessed and deployed in the service of some greater good, some miraculous bargain like the one Johnson made?

Listen to the song.

All will be revealed.

DBC

THE HOXTON CHRISTIAN MISSION

As overheard by DBC Pierre

THE following is how many words it takes a Hackney Cab driver, on a fare from the West End to Hoxton Market, to realise that a couple in the back will nod whether they're listening or not.

Yamazaki? Your hotel doesn't have Yamazaki? I should bloody hope not. Look at all the carnage they done in the war.

Wouldn't wipe me arse with em. I had a pair, not unlike you, in the back of the cab once who also said they was film directors. And I says to em, I says – 'Can't be much cop, if you're still out hailing cabs in the road. Where's your Learjet then?' They laughed. Well, they couldn't say nuffin could they? I mean, take this place you're goin – course it's a bleedin brothel now or summit – the blokes who started that, back when it was the Hoxton Market Christian Mission, right little pair called John and Lewis Burtt, had been picked up off the street covered in shit. And even after all that d'you think they went round cryin for lack of Dolce & Gabbana? No. They was sent to a Ragged School, and scraped clean, you know, back in the day like they did – and when they came out they started doin the same for other nippers sleepin rough. Didn't go out buyin Agas or bloody Smegs all over the place. I know this cos they joined up with lads from Rectory Road Congregational Church in Hackney, where I used to go before I stopped goin. They even started doin meals on wheels, and between em set up this gaff at Hoxton Market in 1886. I know that, it was the year Arsenal FC was founded. And do you think any single one of em woke up of a mornin sayin, 'Let's get a better handbag than the neighbours?' No. NO. Because they had respect. Not like today. The place was stuffed to the rafters with nippers

doin Bible classes and helpin humanity and showin respect. There was so many of em they had to rebuild and expand the place twice, until the Great War, you know, lest we forget. All the lads was shipped out of the country to face the Bosch and not a one of em saw fit to get a bigger head than his comrades. Not a one. And we still came back with a 5–0 victory. Meanwhile this gaff, where you're goin, looked after all their families while they was gone. All the families, just like that. And when the lads was back with the cup they helped em all bugger off to Australia. Assisted emigration they called it. Mind, not as assisted as your first Australians. No, no, you mark my words: respect. They used to make boots here an all, for nippers. Fed the needy, 'Daddy Burtt's for dinner,' they used to say. No stigma on it, not like today.

Course, before you buggers even knew what a Parmesan shaving was we were bombed every night straight. And to our credit we didn't go out and say, 'Let's hide the truffle oil.' D'you know what this mob did? Evacuated the disabled. Got the nippers out to safety. Even got bombed emselves, but did what they had to do, not like today. Ended up they moved out to the seaside, nippers an all. Even survived Harold Wilson in the end.

That'll be £19.80, I can't help roadworks. If you want to know who needs bombing it's the borough council. And a word of advice, my little friends: don't go flouncin round here with your Hugo Boss rubbish. This manor's seen the horrors of war.

You're fuckin joking. That's a fifty – I can't change that.

Jesus wept.

Here – haven't I seen you before?

The Oscars? Gosh, blimey sir, yes. Just a bit of banter, you know? No, no, sir, heaven forbid, no charge at all, couldn't take your money. But here, could you sign this for my nipper? He'll get no end of kudos at school.

✝

AND YOU SHALL KNOW ME BY MY TRAIL OF ONIONS

By Andrew Weatherall

FRIED-ONION aroma assailed, I am the Bisto kid. Drawn by drunken hunger and Svengali curlicues of meat waft. Floating not walking … Fried-onion aroma assailed, I am more than happy to play salmonella roulette. You do know those trolleys are covered in pigeon shit?

'Death dog … sorry … hot dog … with onions, mustard and ketchup.'

Sunrise over the silly-con roundabout. Take me home, Curtain Road … to the overpriced flat where I belong.

Yes, I know that technically I was performing what is now popularly known as the 'walk of shame', but by this stage in my life I liked to think of myself as a professional shame-walker, with certain standards, that no matter how low had to be maintained … standards that in some cases can lessen the shame. And hasten the walk …

ON CONSUMING MEAT PRODUCTS
IN THE STREET
(RULE 3: SUB-SECTION 4: PARAGRAPH 2)

If the public highway being employed is unpeopled then consumption is permitted. However, on observing pedestrians approaching, particularly those half one's age and twice as attractive, any meat product being consumed should be lowered and held out of sight until such time that you are unobserved. NB. Beware of possible droppage …

Although the cashmere Balenciaga overcoat only cost £200 courtesy of a hard-up bugle enthusiast, in real terms it was worth nearer the £1,000 mark … which is why when some hours later, on regaining consciousness, the additional touches of colour provided by Mr French and Mr Heinz were somewhat annoying. The dry cleaning could wait. The hangover, on the other hand …

I've always been a cheap sugar and salt rush kind of man. Never was one for Spooner and Stanshall's 'Dare of the Hog'. Frazzles and Irn Bru … must have Frazzles and Irn Bru …

I opened my front door to start the late afternoon Bru quest and there before me, splatting sporadically like freshly squeezed oil paint topped with glistening onion fragments covering 200 yards of pavement palette, was the evidence of my maintained standards – my adherence to Rule 3: Sub-Section 4: Paragraph 2.

IN MEMORY OF THE PEOPLE OF HOXT
KILLED IN THE SECOND WORLD WA
1939

MEAT MISSION

MEAT MISSION

MEAT MISSION

MEAT MISSION

MEAT MISSION

MEAT MISSION

MEAT MISSION

MEAT MISSION

MEAT MISSION

MEAT MISSION

MEAT MISSION

MEAT MISSION

DEVILLED EGGS

ONE of my favourite drinking snacks, Devilled Eggs have been largely forgotten since the 1970s. They make great party food, but beware – the effects of these on the bowel can be somewhat … dramatic. Steer well clear if you're expecting to get any play that night.

YP

WHAT YOU NEED

18 eggs, hard-boiled and peeled
60ml EVOO (extra virgin olive oil)
2 tbsp mayonnaise
1 tbsp white wine vinegar
1 tbsp Dijon mustard
A pinch of paprika
1 small bunch of chives, finely chopped
Curly parsley for garnish
Salt and pepper to taste

WHAT YOU DO

Cut the eggs in half and remove the yolks.

Choose the best 24 halves and discard the rest.

Arrange the empty halves on a serving plate.

Mix the egg yolks, EVOO, mayonnaise, vinegar and mustard in a bowl together with a pinch of salt, pepper and paprika to taste.

Using a piping bag, fill each egg half with the mixture.

Sprinkle the chives over the top of the eggs and garnish with a sprig of curly parsley for the true '70s experience.

Drink: Melon Balls.

WINGS @ HOME

W E SELL a lot of wings. There are banks of fryers working overtime to get them out to the hungry masses. The grease they generate is phenomenal. At home I'm not a big fan of deep frying – it's too messy, wasteful of oil and the smell lingers for days.

Wings are something you can cook pretty much as well in the oven at home as you can in an industrial fryer. And they are almost embarrassingly easy to do. The baking powder and salt will dry out the skin so you get that all-important crunch rather than a mouthful of flaccid fat.

YP

WHAT YOU NEED

1kg chicken wings, jointed
1tsp baking powder
1tsp salt
250ml Frank's Hot Sauce or similar
250g butter

FOR THE BLUE CHEESE SAUCE
200g mayonnaise
100g sour cream
100g Gorgonzola
2 cloves garlic
15ml white wine vinegar
½ tsp onion powder
10ml lemon juice
A pinch of salt
A pinch of finely ground black pepper

WHAT YOU DO

For the blue cheese sauce: mince the garlic and combine all ingredients except the cheese in a bowl.

Crumble the Gorgonzola into very small pieces and stir into the mayo mix.

Refrigerate and let sit, ideally overnight.

Before serving, taste again and season to taste. You may need a drop more vinegar or lemon juice at this stage, too.

Toss the chicken wings with the salt and the baking powder and refrigerate overnight on a roasting tray.

Roast in the oven on a wire rack at 220 °C for approximately 30 minutes or until golden brown and cooked through, turning halfway through.

Melt the butter over a medium heat in a frying pan or wok and slowly stir in the hot sauce.

Add the wings and toss until thoroughly coated.

Serve with: Blue Cheese Sauce and ice-cold beer.

(over the page)
NAME: Alice
DRINK: leftovers
MEMORY: better than yours

KOREAN FRIED CHICKEN

Courtesy of Gizzi Erskine

THE first time I made Korean Fried Chicken was about six years ago. My chef friend Judy Joo, who is a Korean New Yorker, was explaining the ways of 'the other KFC' when we were working together filming a show. I was off to New York that month and she insisted I took a trip to Korea Town to try some fried chicken wings. Before I go she gives me a recipe to try. Clueless about the ingredients and feeling a bit lazy, I swap some of them for what I think are British variations. My first Korean Fried Chicken is good but nothing like the real deal I get when I hit up K-Town in NYC.

I work in the States loads, and whether I'm in Los Angeles, San Francisco or New York I always take a trip to K-Town to have some wings. Fast-forward six years, the recipe has been developed about a thousand times and it's now (I guess) my signature dish. It makes an appearance at pretty much every event, takeover or pop-up I do, though I've never fully published it before. I am writing this recipe while in Seoul and for the first time feel like I can finally put it to bed after having mountains of the stuff from its motherland and knowing that, for sure, I have it right.

My recipe is a fusion of American meets Asian, brining the wings first in a buttermilk brine to tenderise, season and firm them up. They are then tossed in a blend of three flours. You might think this step is a bit extreme, but each one does its own thing. Self-raising (wheat flour) is for puff, potato is for chew and rice flour gives it crunch. Don't mess about with this step. The wings are then confited on a low heat until cooked, then dried and flash-fried making them crisp and drawing out the juices to form an umami crust. Finally

they are tossed in an addictive Korean chilli sauce, then coated in sesame seeds and very finely sliced spring onions to garnish. Serve them the Korean way over the American, piled into mountains alongside a stack of imported beer while watching football or K-pop with pals.

WHAT YOU NEED

Serves 4

8 free-range or organic chicken wings, wing tips cut off then cut in half through the joint to make 16 pieces

FOR THE BRINE
200ml buttermilk
1 tbsp salt

FOR THE SAUCE
2 tbsp Gochujang Korean red pepper paste
2 tbsp Sriracha Thai chilli sauce
4 tbsp caster sugar
4 tbsp rice wine vinegar
2 tbsp ketchup
1 tbsp sesame oil
1 tbsp butter or chicken fat/schmaltz

FLOUR MIX
4 tbsp self-raising flour
2 tbsp rice flour
2 tbsp potato flour
Salt and white pepper
2 tbsp toasted sesame seeds, white, black or both
2 spring onions, the green part only, very thinly sliced (Japanese style so not on a slant)
Salt and Pepper

WHAT YOU DO

Mix the buttermilk and salt together, massage it into the chicken wings and leave in the fridge for 12–24 hours.

To make the sauce: melt together the Gochujang, Sriracha, sugar, vinegar, ketchup, sesame oil and butter. Bring to the boil for a minute, then turn off the heat and set aside.

Mix all the flours together in a bowl and season well. Take the wings out of the buttermilk, wiping any excess off them and toss them 4 pieces by 4 pieces in the flour mixture.

Heat the oil to 140 °C in either a deep fat fryer or a deep pan or wok filled ⅓ up its sides with oil. Fry gently (or confit) the wings for 8–10 minutes or until they are cooked through but have barely taken on any colour. Remove the wings from the fryer and drain on kitchen paper.

Turn up your fryer to 190 °C and fry the wings for 2–3 minutes or until you get a golden colour. Drain, dry again on kitchen paper and then toss the wings in the sauce and 1 tbsp of the sesame seeds and then plate. Sprinkle over the rest of the sesame seeds and the spring onions and serve immediately with cold beer.

CURRYWURST

FAST FOOD IN ZE FAST LANE

BLITZING down the Autobahn, limiter working overtime – 155 mph, knuckles white and jaw clenched, eyes wide and face contorted into rictus by adrenaline. Foot jammed to the floor for hours now, half-mad from the incessant whine of the turbochargers.*

The final leg of a three-day expedition which has taken us from a biker gathering in Sealand via a jungle rave in Bremen and now onto a summer shooting party at Hermann Goering's old summer house in the leafy suburbs of Berlin.

An amber light winks into life on the dashboard, ordering me to stop for fuel.

At these speeds the big V8 drinks a lot.

As does my travelling kompanion: he's a nervous passenger at the best of times but the past 48 hours have broken him. He has at least pushed through the panicked and terrified screaming into some kind of inebriated shellshock and so now is mercifully silent.

Polizei power past; a sign appears, advertising a Rasthof.

I order my foot to ease off the accelerator pedal and our speed begins to fall.

We're still doing 90 when we hit the off-ramp, rumble strips threatening to shake the fillings right out of our teeth. The engine screams down through the gears, shrieking like a Stuka, the car shedding speed fast. Finally the big German auto comes to a HALT! by a petrol pump.

I set about uncurling my fingers from the steering wheel.

My travelling kompanion sets about uncurling his from an empty bottle of Fürst Bismarck.†

Having refuelled our Wagen we go hunting for our own fix in the car park, forgoing the diverse selection of exotic foodstuffs on offer in the main Raststätte,‡ we head for where the real action is – a cluster of fellow addicts huddled together under a red and black flag. You can smell their shame from here. And their mullets.

I make eye contact with the dealer. My fingers single 'two'. He nods, Teutonically, then turns to his wares to prepare our order.

A wurst is inserted into a sausage slicer – the Germans consider knives to be far too inefficient a way to kut stuff nowadays – and in two seconds a dozen perfectly even chunks of sausage are deposited onto a pile of pommes frites waiting on a paper plate below.

A good soaking with kurry sauce and a sprinkling of kurry powder complete the dish.

'ACHTUNG! ENGLÄNDER!'

He thrust ze wursts towards us.

In my mind's eye, motorbikes sail over barbed-wire fences …

Deutschmarks change hands and the two of us fall on the food like a pair of Schweinehunde, skewering chunks of sausage and sodden chips with tiny plastic forks and mashing them into our maws.

Minuten later, kravings sated but klothes und faces sullied by sauce, ve skveeze ourselves back into ze Audi, und eyes hooded from the initial effects of ein Fleischkoma ve kontinue our journey.

At 70 mph. In ze slow lane.

Although the Germans lay claim to this dish and it is generally accepted that Herta Heuwer was the first person to sell Kurrywurst from her stand in Charlottenburg in 1949, she herself admitted that she was given the ingredients, (ketchup, curry powder and Worcestershire sauce) by British squaddies.

You're welcome, Germany. You're welcome.

YP

---

* All I have to listen to since the stereo becoming permanently stuck on a Rammstein CD just outside of Hamburg, and my kompanion finally succumbing to a minor breakdown somewhere around Rendsburg.

† A common brand of Korn – a particularly noxious spirit drunk by Germans who can't afford bleach.

‡ Schnitzel mit Kartoffeln, Schnitzel mit Reis, Schnitzel mit Pommes Frites oder das Special: Nudeln mit Schnitzel. In German there is no word for salad. Fact.

WHAT YOU NEED

2 Bratwurst or Currywurst
250ml tomato ketchup
1 tsp Worcestershire sauce
2 tbsp mild cheap curry powder
Vegetable oil for frying

WHAT YOU DO

Cut the wurst into 3cm-thick slices.

Heat a small amount of vegetable oil in a frying pan over a low heat. Add the wurst and fry slowly until the skins are starting to crisp slightly.

Mix together the ketchup, Worcestershire sauce and most of the curry powder, then add to the pan and stir well, ensuring all pieces of wurst are coated with the sauce. Continue to cook for 1 minute.

Remove the wurst from the pan and place on top of a plate of French fries. Pour the sauce over the top and sprinkle the remaining curry powder over the top.

Serve with: a second portion of Kurrywurst.

Drink: ice-cold Pilsner.

Listen to: 'Du Hast' by Rammstein (or the theme from *The Great Escape*).

SNOW BLIND

Courtesy of Giles Looker

THE White Russian/Snow Blind. The problem with such a simple drink is that all bartenders think theirs is the best. Not true. The White Russian consistently tastes and looks different every time due to being made with different ingredients. It started life as the Barbara: 2 parts vodka, 1 part crème de cacao, 1 part cream. It was not until the 1960s that people swapped the cacao for Kahlúa and the White Russian was born. It was made even more popular in the 1990s because of The Dude in *The Big Lebowski*, where it was called a 'Caucasian'. The beauty of this drink is the deceptive punch of alcohol it carries. It is one of the easiest and tastiest drinks to consume.

WHAT YOU NEED

25ml vodka
25ml Kahlúa
50ml half and half (equal quantities of whole milk and double cream)

NO GARNISH
'Hold the fucking gardening'

WHAT YOU DO

Place all the ingredients into a cocktail shaker, shake over cubed ice and then pour into a 12oz old-fashioned glass over cubed ice.

At MEATliquor we sometimes rim the old-fashioned glass with desiccated coconut. This is often known as the Snow Blind. DRINK.

```
*************************************

       ALPHONSO
    WINGMAN OF GOD

*************************************

REQUIEM MASS IN D MINOR -
  W. A. MOZART
```

REVELATIONS

THE REVELATIONS OF PIERRE THE INTEMPERATE

THE MEATliquor CHRONICLES
PART TEN

777 words (mentor of the Beast)

WHAT the Bible needed: a summary. Back to the studio to wrap up action between demons and saints. Some estimates put the death toll from God in the Bible at 33 million, and the toll from the devil at two. But in this book there was no toll unless self-inflicted, and the demons and saints were equals. Who are demons after all but disgruntled saints? Who are saints but naive demons? They all saw a shine and made it holy; we saw a shine and used the notion of them to suggest it's holy too.

So what really went on in these pages? Some might say burgers, booze and a glib blasphemy. But it's not about the burger, and it's not blasphemous. The position of these chronicles is that we're fucking doomed. Doomed as a people and as an idea. Freedom is doomed, reason is doomed; unless we start opting out, unless we gather around the free and the good, around Quality, around things that emphasise a need to make judgements from scratch, that advertise a right to fail and recover by ourselves. It may seem a lot of meaning to stand behind a burger, but it's right to start small and let the thing speak for itself; the cities we live in have new and trendy restaurants with buzzwords for names and decor by Osmond Lalalala that serve dry turd and goat's cheese paninis with a warm wine for thirty quid. It's not incredible anymore that we live in a killing field of Quality, now evolved to a microbacterial level; it's incredible that everyone flocks to it like fucking zombies.

Without the ability to discern between the real and imaginary we are fucking doomed. So look around us: we are fucking doomed.

How much of what we're encouraged to eat and think and do is bullshit? A majority. That's what brings the characters in this book together. And see how the cultural immune system deals with them: by colouring them demons, mavericks, outlaws and bad boys. Because they feel that all the shit we're supposed to think is wrong. Because they think the new gaming station that reads irises and sends behavioural details for analysis and targeting is fucking sinister. Because they don't believe it's designed to serve the consumer; because they think anyone who falls for such a con is a fucking zombie, because they know in their hearts that it's just another sinister finger up the ass. Because they know zombies now run the show, and they're breeding an even dumber batch.

Will we stand here at the foot of the hill and watch it grow? Will we let a place engulf us where every transaction is a trick, every enticement a lie, where the only visible curve is declining Quality?

We already did that.

If today isn't a reason to drink, get creative and get real, nothing will ever be.

So this book is about what happens when people grow tired and refuse to have fingers up their asses. The banks, the snacks, the accessories, the e-shit, the coffees, the insurers, the bureaucrats can all stick their fingers up their own asses. The book is about living with an ass empty of uninvited fingers, with veins empty of drip-feeds and guts free of catheters. Does it mean we think we're doing you a favour? No. The market wants you to feel it's doing you a favour, not us. Do we think you're doing us a favour? No. And that's the thing: we're zero sums together, equals for the most obvious reasons; and if ever in history there was a fucking hill before us to climb, we're at the foot of it now.

You can say it's a lot of noise about meat and drinks. Yes, it is, just that; but the noise applies to everything. So what comes next?

This: with book in hand, we're fed and watered ready for a climb. We can see the hill, towering alongside. Do we run from it or to it? Let's run to it, with all our hellish energies. Let's meet, conspire and rise up, for we have glimpsed a promised land. We can have it, build it from scratch.

Gather your Hellhounds.

Let's go forth and multiply.

I got to keep movin', I got to keep movin'
Blues fallin' down like hail, blues fallin' down like hail;
Mmm, blues fallin' down like hail, blues fallin' down
  like hail;
And the days keeps on worryin' me,
There's a hellhound on my trail,
Hellhound on my trail, hellhound on my trail …

I can tell the wind is risin',
The leaves tremblin' on the tree …

DBC

BOURGEOIS HORS D'OEUVRES

Courtesy of DBC Pierre

ONE of the lessons of the hill is that certain of your fellow hillhounds can stray too far to get laid, and a moment then arrives when you find yourself on the outskirts of a clique that talks about Audi convertibles and villa holidays in Tuscany. The protocol here is not to abandon the hillhound – forgive his poor choice as far as you can, but demonstrate to the clique their actual place in the hierarchy.

WHAT YOU NEED

1 cucumber
1 small pot of crème fraiche
1 bunch of baby carrot-top greens
1 block of Parmesan cheese
24 vol-au-vent cases
1 jar of finest red pesto
2 tins of 'value range' mushy peas
1 shopping bag, preferably Eco

WHAT YOU DO

Fill the vol-au-vent cases with as much mushy-pea mix as possible, packing down with a teaspoon to achieve maximum capacity and a flat top.

Arrange all on a baking tray and warm in a pre-heated oven at 180 °C for 6 minutes.

While the stealth bombs cook, shave fine slices of Parmesan with a potato peeler, and finely slice 24 cucumber rounds.

Place a cucumber round on each case as a lid, top with a blob of sour cream, parmesan shavings and a flourish of red pesto.

Artfully garnish with a sprig of carrot greens, and casually toss the Waitrose bag in full view for added sense of security. Then wait.

Three hours after consumption, declare the bathroom out of use, remove the dog from the room, turn off all music and watch gleefully, for hours of suburban enjoyment.

ROAST BEEF SUNDAE

A S A child of the late '70s and early '80s the Knickerbocker Glory was the pinnacle in dessert technology. Finishing one of these was almost a rite of passage. The spectacle of the presentation always brought a sense of wonder to any nearby child. The Roast Beef Sundae takes what can often be a very formal meal and makes it fun: baby food for adults in the best possible way.

YP

THE SUNDAE

TOPPING
4 cherry tomatoes
Maldon sea salt

Sprinkle with Maldon sea salt and roast at 180 °C until just wrinkling. Leave stems intact.

HORSERADISH *from a jar (gasp!)*

CARAMELISED ONIONS
2 large onions
Olive oil
A splash of balsamic vinegar
Maldon sea salt

Heat a good slug of olive oil in a large frying pan over a low heat. Add sliced onions and a pinch of sea salt and cook slowly, stirring occasionally, for 15 minutes, or until onions have started to turn golden brown. Add vinegar and continue to cook, stirring, until onions are sticky and caramelised.

MASHED POTATOES
4 medium-sized potatoes
50ml full-cream milk
50ml double cream
40g salted butter
½ tsp Maldon sea salt
½ tsp each white and black pepper
A pinch of nutmeg
1 tsp balsamic vinegar

Peel and boil the potatoes in salted water until they start to fall apart when picked up with a fork. Drain, then leave in the colander to steam off while you add the milk, white pepper, black pepper and nutmeg to the (now empty) potato pan and warm gently, but do not boil. Mash the potatoes into the milk, then add the butter, cream, vinegar and salt. Adjust seasoning to taste. Stir/mash well until there are no lumps and everything is incorporated. The consistency should be creamy – forming peaks without becoming 'gluey'.

ROAST BEEF
500g rump roast
Maldon sea salt
Black pepper
Thyme

Season with salt, pepper and thyme, and roast until rare at 180 °C (around 25 minutes). Sear the outside in a smoking-hot heavy frying pan. Cover with foil and allow to cool. Refrigerate. To serve, slice *very* thinly, and heat in the gravy.

BOTTOM
4 cherry tomatoes
Maldon sea salt

Sprinkle with Maldon sea salt and roast at 180 °C until just wrinkling. Remove stems.

Arrange in layers in an ice-cream sundae glass.

MEAT GRAVY

STAGE 1
4 onions (peeled, halved)
3 carrots (halved)
3 stalks celery
1 parsnip (halved)
2 cloves garlic (unpeeled)
Beef shin bones (cut into sections or cracked)
500g (approx.) beef shin
Salt and pepper

On a lightly oiled baking tray, form a trivet of the vegetables and place the beef shin and bones on top. Season and roast at 170 °C for an hour or until the vegetables are nicely caramelised. Remove most of the marrow from the bones and set aside for later.

STAGE 2
4 onions (peeled, halved)
3 carrots (halved)
3 stalks celery
1 tbsp peppercorns
1 bay leaf

Add the bones and roast meat from Stage 1 to a large stockpot together with the vegetables, the peppercorns and the bay leaf. Cover with cold water and simmer for 2 hours, skimming any scum from the surface of the water. Strain into a saucepan and discard the solid matter, retaining the stock, which should be full of beefy umami.

STAGE 3
Remove the skins from the previously roasted garlic and add to a saucepan, together with all the other roasted vegetables. Deglaze the roasting pan over a hob with a splash of white wine, scraping off all the crunchy bits stuck to the bottom. When the bottom of the roasting tray has been cleaned, add the liquid to the pan of vegetables. Top up with cold water and simmer for 20 minutes. With a stick blender, blend everything into a soupy sludge and press through a sieve with the back of a spoon, making sure all the liquid has been squeezed out. The remaining liquid should be full of caramelised sweetness. If it tastes 'thin', simmer the liquid for a while until it has reduced a little and intensified in flavour.

STAGE 4
In a large saucepan start by adding half of the beef stock and half of the vegetable stock. Bring to the boil and taste. Add more of each of the two stocks, tasting continuously until the gravy flavours are balanced to your satisfaction. Simmer and reduce until slightly thinner than your desired final consistency. If necessary, thicken to taste by adding a small amount of butter/flour roux and incorporating well. Whisk the marrow from Stage 1 into the warm gravy just before serving, *then* adjust seasoning to taste.

Serve in a jug alongside the Sundae with Yorkshire puddings and a bib.

THE LITERARY AGENCY
12 GETHSEMANE MEWS
NW3 2FU

20 June 2014

Yianni Papoutsis, Esq.
Scott Collins, Esq.
c/o MEATliquor
74 Welbeck Street
London W1G OBA

Dear Yianni and Scott

It is with great regret that I am writing to terminate our agreement, so I am giving you the requisite thirty days' notice. After that period has elapsed I will no longer act as your literary agent, although I will continue to collect any monies that come through to you until you make alternative arrangements. Please acknowledge receipt of this letter as soon as possible.

There are a number of reasons for this, as you are no doubt aware. Your behaviour, particularly at meetings with publishers, has been downright diabolical. We pride ourselves on being a friendly, tolerant bunch, but a number of people have been shocked by your rudeness, not least myself. I recall that particular incident at Shoreditch House involving a highly regarded editor with horror. You have delivered material late and do not seem to understand that deadlines are just that. In fact, it is a miracle that anyone has agreed to publish this book, in my humble opinion.

I wish you all the best with your future endeavours.

Diana Beaumont (Ms)
Literary Agent

PS. Have you ever considered expanding your menu so that there are more options available for vegetarians or those who are gluten intolerant? Food for thought!

Subject: MEATliquor Chronicles

From: Dave Watkins <davidwatkins@faber.com>
To: Lee Brackstone <leebrackstone@faber.com>

28 July 2014 14:32

Dear Lee

You know, I hope, that I enjoy my work. I try to be a diligent and resourceful editor, courteous and sensitive to the needs of my authors while maintaining the necessary discipline to see a book through with the minimum of fuss.

When you announced that we would be publishing *The MEATliquor Chronicles*, I was, in spite of some initial bemusement as to what constitutes a 'burger pioneer', genuinely excited to be working on the project.

Here, in no particular order, are some of the things I have learnt in the course of editing *The MEATliquor Chronicles*:

- It is a very specific kind of personality that chooses a nocturnal career in a high-pressure sweatbox
- The *London Review of Books* café is not always the most appropriate venue for an emergency scheduling meeting
- The threat of bodily harm is, contrary to Faber's HR guidelines, a very effective motivator
- It is possible to drink yourself sober

Having now approved the book for press, it is with some small regret – and a renewed appreciation for the works of Ernest Hemingway – that I must inform you I have requested a transfer to the poetry department.

Best

Dave

—

Dave Watkins
Editor, Faber & Faber

Re: Subject: MEATliquor Chronicles

From: Lee Brackstone <leebrackstone@faber.com>   **28 July 2014 14:40**
To: Dave Watkins <davidwatkins@faber.com>

Dear Dave

Thanks for yours. The past decade or so in publishing has seen the tectonic plates of our industry shift, and the business is now unrecognisable from the one I started in some 18 years ago, as a young man, setting T. S. Eliot's fires at Faber. Ebooks. Amazon. Metadata. Discoverability. These are the buzzwords of the day, and I fear we've lost something of the Corinthian spirit that informs great publishing along the way.

But I have to say, nothing shocks and disappoints me more than your supine, spineless surrender at the hands of these reprehensible hedonists. As a man schooled in the ancient publishing art of 'the long lunch', I can only say you have let the side down (and yourself), badly. Publishers and chefs should have much in common, as both are engaged in an alchemical experiment with content, form and appetite. It saddens me to see you crushed in this battle of alcoholic wills. Oh how I mourn the passing of the five-bottle lunch . . .

Lee

Lee Brackstone
Publisher, Faber & Faber

BROWN BUTTER STEAK & EGGS

Hosted by DBC Pierre

ALTHOUGH this recipe can be enjoyed throughout life, like all good weapons it has a specific application.

Timeline: 8.40 a.m. Location: unknown to anyone concerned. Two bodies in shades and Hawaiian shirts are propped across a desk. They faintly resemble Yianni and Pierre.

'Arghh! What are all those things?'

'Flowers,' croaks Yianni.

'Are we dead?'

'Pull your head away from the window. It must be the garden. And pass the whisky if you're going to fucking shout like that.'

'I can't see any whisky.'

'Then we are dead.'

'I wondered, because the room has no window. Is this a hangover?' Pierre checks his limbs, satisfied that all six are intact.

Yianni lowers his shades, addressing the ashtray: 'It can't be a hangover: we haven't slept yet.'

'Things are looking grim if this is still yesterday. Do you think the ambulance will come out if we pay them this time?'

'We could give them next door's address. Or a better idea: ever hear of meat, carbs, fat and salt?'

'Never got into disco.'

'God, you're fucking gone. Take hold of my belt and follow me – if my calculations are correct, this central air duct must lead through the roof to a kitchen.'

'This one? It's a cigar box.'

'Good idea, bring cigars. I will cure you, my friend …'

WHAT YOU NEED

Serves 1

100g fillet steak
250g butter
2 eggs
1 thick slice of white bread
Salt and pepper

WHAT YOU DO

Salt the steak thoroughly and leave, uncovered, in the fridge for an hour.

Scrape away any salt left visible on the steak and pat dry with a paper towel.

Crack one egg into a teacup, and add just the yolk of the second, discarding the second egg white.

In a heavy frying pan (preferably cast iron), heat 75g of butter until it has melted and started to go brown. Give the steak a good grind of black pepper then fry quickly in the pan. This should only take a minute or so per side. Remove the steak and set aside to rest. Add another 75g butter to the pan and when this starts to brown, tip the pan slightly so that the butter pools and gently lower the eggs into the butter. They should cook very quickly – remove them as soon as the whites have cooked while the yolks are still runny.

Add the remaining butter to the pan and fry the bread until golden brown on both sides.

Serve with any remaining butter poured over the steak.

Drink: Red Snapper and black coffee.

Wear: sunglasses.

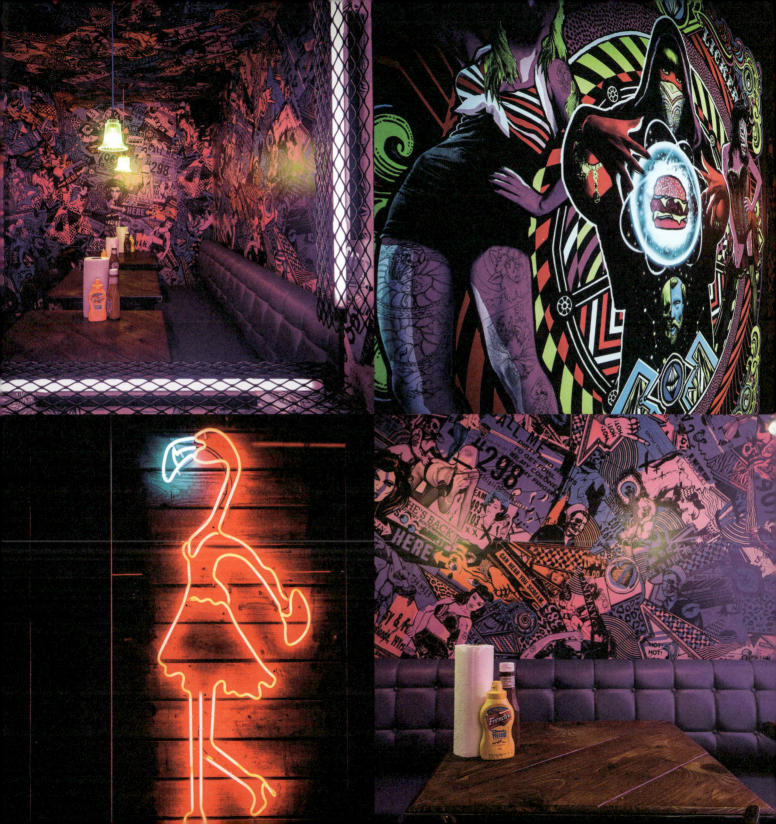

www.meattransmission.com

RADIO RULES

NO COLDPLAY // NO BEATLES

NO CELINE DION // NO MORRISSEY

NO BIEBER // NO ENYA

NO SHIRTCOCKING // NO HIPPIES

NO BONGOS // NO SPORTS

NO EXCEPTIONS

IT'S NOT WHAT YOU SAY, IT'S WHAT YOU PLAY

SHUT THE FUCK UP AND PLAY SOME MUSIC

THE 3 Rs: RAUCOUS, RELENTLESS, ROWDY

TANTANMEN RAMEN

Courtesy of Ross Shonhan, Bone Daddies

SCOTT and Yianni have been great supporters of ours since we opened, and when they asked us to contribute to this project we saw it as a continuation of that support. A lot of people do cookbooks for arrogance and ego but I think these guys are just doing it for a bit of fun.

WHAT IS RAMEN?
Ramen = Delicious

WHAT IS BONE DADDIES?
Home of the big long noodle

The world of ramen is endless. Any bone, any veg, any meat, any flavour can go into ramen; chefs in Japan make Thai curry ramen, tomato ramen, cheese ramen … to name but a few. It's a freedom ramen chefs have in Japan that other styles of traditional food don't really allow.

Bone Daddies Ramen was born of a dream to make no-bullshit honest tasty ramen noodles in London.

We never had a plan to transplant a part of Japan to Soho; we wanted to create something new – London Style Rock and Roll Ramen.

If you don't like beer, ramen or rock and roll then this is not your place. I love Soho because you don't have to try to please everyone. We play classic rock and roll, and came up with the idea that it had to be 20 years or older to stop anyone in the team thinking it was OK to play Britney Spears.

We do bowls that make us smile and hopefully make other people smile, too.

WHAT YOU NEED

Serves 4

FOR THE STOCK
Make 1.25l of strong chicken stock, but add fresh ginger, konbu, dried shiitakes and leek instead of mirepoix. Or buy a good quality stock and flavour with the veggies above.

FOR THE SESAME TARE
200g roasted white sesame seeds
150g soy sauce
100g sugar
100ml chilli oil
35g ginger (peeled and roughly chopped)
20g spring onion
250g sesame paste

Place all in a food processor and blend till smooth.

FOR THE MINCED PORK
200g minced pork
20g tobanjan
160g soy
5g chilli oil
5g vegetable oil
5g garlic (peeled, finely chopped)
5g ginger (peeled, finely chopped)
10g spring onion (finely chopped)

Stir-fry pork in hot vegetable oil till brown then add all other ingredients and cook till dry.

FOR THE EGGS
4 eggs (soft-boiled, peeled)
100ml soy sauce
100ml water
10g sugar

Mix all together then marinate the eggs overnight if possible, but for at least 3–4 hours.

200g cooked bamboo (canned and drained or vacuum packed)
5g sesame oil
100g soy
10g sugar
2g chilli flakes

Stir-fry the bamboo in the sesame oil till dry then add remaining ingredients. Cook until dry.

110g fresh noodles (find a good quality ramen noodle or
  replace with another noodle)
4 large bok choy leaves (blanched and chilled)
200g bean sprouts (blanched)
20g chives (thinly sliced)
Chilli oil (make your own or buy a good quality one)

WHAT YOU DO

Prepare all the ingredients above and have them laid out ready to use quickly. Set up a pot to heat the stock and another with boiling water to cook your noodles.

Cook the noodles and drain.

Divide the tare between the four bowls and pour the hot stock evenly into them.

Whisk until the tare has made the stock creamy.

Divide the noodles between the four bowls.

Top with bean sprouts, bamboo, egg, minced pork, bok choy, and chives.

Finally, finish with as much chilli oil as you dare!

IBÉRICO PORK MEATBALLS WITH CUTTLEFISH

Courtesy of José Pizarro

I LOVE meatballs! They are my favourite comfort food and so versatile. My mum used to make meatballs. Pork and beef was her speciality, with an onion sauce. I was a cheeky boy back then – trying to steal the meatballs from the pan before she put in the sauce. These days I'm better behaved around meatballs.

These particular meatballs are very popular in my restaurants. I use Ibérico pork, of course – the most amazing pork on this earth. Its unique nutty flavour makes it very special. If you cannot get your hands on some Ibérico pork, then use one of those old UK breeds that are full of flavour, like Tamworth or Old Spot.

Mixing meat and fish is a very Catalan thing. Cuttlefish not only balances the flavours here, but also the budget. Enjoy!

WHAT YOU NEED

FOR THE MEATBALLS
1kg pork mince
6g salt
20g chopped garlic
1 large egg
12g breadcrumbs
5g freshly ground black pepper
6g parsley
40g pancetta, finely chopped
20g olive oil
35g bread soaked in milk
100g plain flour for rolling
Olive oil for frying

FOR THE CUTTLEFISH
1.5kg cuttlefish, cleaned and cut into small cubes
3 tbsp olive oil
1 large onion, diced
6 large tomatoes, deseeded, peeled and finely chopped
1.5l fish stock
A good handful of chopped flat-leaf parsley

WHAT YOU DO

Mix all the ingredients for the meatballs together and make your balls by taking a good pinch of mix, rolling between your palms, then coating each one with flour.

Fry them in plenty of olive oil.

In another pan heat the 3 tbsps of olive oil, and fry the cuttlefish until each piece starts to change colour.

Remove from the oil and set to one side.

In the same pan add the onions and fry until they caramelise.

Add the tomatoes and fry until all the juices have evaporated.

Add the cooked cuttlefish and the fish stock, bring to the boil and simmer for 15 minutes.

Lastly add the meatballs and bring to the boil.

Plate up immediately with a good scattering of chopped parsley and devour.

GAME OVER

Courtesy of Giles Looker

THE early-morning sun lasers though the smoke into bloodshot eyes.

Half-naked, all drunk and covered in ash, our hero crouches amid the devastation and pours the last drops from a bottle of bourbon into a smudged and dirty glass. The solid foodstuffs ran out a long time ago.

Discarded canisters of green, toxic-looking, stimulant-laced sugar water litter the vicinity.

Groping around, he finds one with some liquid left in it and tops up his drink.

A nearby artillery strike shakes the room as he lifts the precious fuel to his lips. He doesn't spill a drop: the sound of exploding ordnance is just background noise now. In many ways he finds it soothing.

A half-smoked spliff rescued from an overflowing ashtray takes the edge off things as the drugs kick in: the stimulants and the liquor pulling his mind in opposite directions but somehow back into fighting shape; the weed steadying his hand. Can't kill shit if you can't shoot straight.

Nerves thrumming, palms sweating, adrenaline pumping, he shakes some life back into his aching trigger-finger.

Time to get back in the fight, soldier.

Time to scratch that primal itch.

Time to kill.

DRINK. Picking up his gun he moves to where a window used to be, staying low to avoid the other snipers. He peeks over the rubble, his eyes scanning the ruins of distant buildings for his prey: the spotter for those damned howitzers.

Somewhere an alarm sounds. Piercing and insistent, it cuts through even the deafening roar of the big guns.

Our hero never wavers from his duty, his eye glued to the scope of his rifle.

Our hero never hears the door open behind him.

Our hero never hears the figure padding into the room.

He is perfectly focused on his hunt.

She is standing right behind him now.

She reaches out, grabs his head and turns his face towards her, tired eyes overflowing with contempt and anger.

'For fuck's sake! Have you been playing that sodding game all night again? How old are you? You need to be at work in an hour and you stink of whisky.'

Shit. Our hero is in trouble.

Again.

YP

WHAT YOU NEED

12.5ml vodka
12.5ml gin
12.5ml tequila
12.5ml rum
12.5ml triple sec
12.5ml Pisang Ambon
A dash of absinthe
20ml lemon juice
10ml gomme
20ml apple purée
Mountain Dew

GARNISH
Lemon juice and maraschino cherry

WHAT YOU DO

Place ingredients into a Boston shaker (except the Mountain Dew). Shake and pour into a tankard glass over cubed ice. Top with Mountain Dew and garnish. DRINK.

Apologise.

✝

THANKS

To the carnivores who ate our meat …

To the drinkers who imbibed our liquor …

To the critics and detractors who inspired us to improve …

To the vegetarians we turned and to the ones we didn't …

… and to all the other collaborators and conspirators, to the friends and family, to the cooks and the crooks, the Burgerettes and the bartenders who supported us and put up with our shit to make all this happen:

Thank you all.

Everything we've ever done was out of love, honesty and happy accidents.

The weighty tome you hold in your hands would never have made it into print without the patience, silent suffering and moral turpitude of the following degenerates: DBC Pierre, Giles Looker, Diana Beaumont, Stephen Page, Lee Brackstone, Dave Watkins, Paul Winch-Furness, Alex Kirby, Luke Bird, Friederike Huber, Jack Murphy, Gemma Lovett, Dan Papps, Sofia Johansson, Dan 'Plon' Gendara, Ian Duff, Scott's mum, The Gaztronome, Zak Whalley, Shed, I Love Dust, W Communications, Huey Morgan and all the other contributors.

✝

CONTRIBUTORS

Alfonso, the Wingman of God is a lieutenant deity for those who have grown tired of unanswered prayers. Easier to access than God, with an average waiting time of only 28 minutes, he handles all the same matters except for those pertaining to sodomy, which have their own dedicated hotline via Saint Sergius. A select group of otherwise pragmatic people, who acknowledge the existence of Heaven and Hell due to experiences with whisky, now appeal first to Alfonso; because he's mortal, and understands mortal concerns, and because he dispenses brutal truth, which is more useful than a few Hail Marys. Alfonso can only be addressed from roads, kerbsides and pavements, and will not answer anyone who worships him, or who can no longer pronounce simple words. A cold, freshly opened beer in a can will often bring him around. He is best appealed to at the beginning of a session, or after, in the dusk of a hangover. A note for new disciples: he judges all matters to do with women as the man's fault. Full stop.

Petra Barran began in the mobile food business in 2005 when she hit the streets with Choc Star, Britain's only dedicated chocolate van. She fell in love with the road, the community and with selling chocolate to people all over London and beyond. The next move forward was to consolidate this to create more opportunities for traders to trade and outside eaters to eat. She co-founded East Street in 2009 and then moved on to found KERB in 2012 – with an MSc in Urban Studies from UCL informing and developing her interest in the spaces of food in cities. Petra was named 'One of the Ten People Who Changed the World' by the *Independent* in 2011, and in 2014 the *Sunday Times* wrote 'Barran has changed the face of British cuisine'.

I'm called **Bates**. Not even my wife calls me by my first name, so as far as you're concerned, no, I don't have one. I hail from South Carolina, the Deep South of the good ol' U.S.-of-A., and I've spent the past 13 years of my life in kitchens and breweries. Since the age of five, shortly after growing my first powerful beard, I've been cutting up everything that runs, swims or flies, and cooking them in all manner of ways; but most happily as whole animals, still struggling and squealing over a wood fire. On busy days I sometimes even forgets to take the leash or saddle off of some of 'em. I've also made beer and liquor in professional settings as well as for 'recreational use', devoting my life to the pursuit of whole-animal-usage, including women, and beautiful, unique beer and spirits, including some you can smoke. Then Yianni visited me one night a couple of years back and the last fucken thing I remember is going to sleep in sunny Charleston and waking up Shanghaied and married in fucken London where I now reside. Motherfucker.

Joe Beef, is a small restaurant in Little Burgundy, Montreal. Their book, *The Art of Living According to Joe Beef*, was published by Ten Speed Press in 2011.

Stefan Chomka is currently the editor of *Restaurant* magazine and has been writing about food and drink for over a decade across numerous titles. During this time he has fought bears in Finland, tangled with fish in the Ukraine, and wrestled with his own feelings of loathing towards pies that aren't self-contained; he has a missing finger, body scars and an ever-expanding waistline by way of proof. His fondest food memory dates back to 1984 when, as a young lad, he coerced his mother to make him chocolate-coated chips after a misunderstanding over a Maryland cookie advert. He is still waiting patiently for Heston Blumenthal to call to discuss the recipe. Stefan lives with his wife and two children in an unspecified location that definitely isn't the south coast of England, has an IQ of 137, an inside leg measurement of 31, and a pathological fear of penguins. He is Piscean by birth but a Taurus by trade. He has no shoe size.

Will Dean is the editor of the *Independent* magazine. He previously worked on the *Independent*'s features desk and on the *Guardian Guide*, before a protracted spell at Her Majesty's pleasure after becoming convinced a wormhole existed on the southbound platform at Clapham North station. In trying to shake that stigma he spent a week being humiliated by the makers of London's second-best burger (cit. the *London Evening Standard*), who went on to learn that his only previous experience in fast food was a two-year spell at various branches of Pizza Hut in the North-West. In 2003 he was named 'Customer Maniac of the Year' at the chain's popular Oldham branch, an achievement he is yet to surpass. The wormhole is still active.

Food writer, pop-up chef, *Sunday Times* magazine columnist and sometime food-telly host, **Gizzi Erskine** worked as a chef in many of London's top restaurants after graduating from the prestigious Leith's School of Food and Wine. She went on to win the BBC *Good Food* magazine prize, and this led her to her becoming a writer and food stylist to some of the country's best chefs, as well as providing regular columns to magazines such as *InStyle*, *Company* and *Arena*. Missing the chaos of working in kitchens, Gizzi started to hold small pop-up events, and now, after her writing, the pop-up side of her business is where she gets her kicks. Gizzi is considered a visionary when it comes to emerging scenes and food trends. Her books to date are the international bestseller *Cook Yourself Thin*, *Kitchen Magic* and most recently the hugely successful and award-winning *Skinny Weeks and Weekend Feasts*. Her hair has its own postcode.

Helen Graves is a food writer based in Peckham, South East London. She is the author of *101 Sandwiches* and *Cook Your Date into Bed*. She has written for the *Guardian*, *The Times* and the *Evening Standard*, and she authors two acclaimed food blogs, *Food Stories* and *The London Review of Sandwiches*. Her writing and recipes are inspired by the diversity of Peckham, and she is a sandwich and jerk-chicken addict. She spent six years perfecting her recipe for jerk marinade, which is available to buy via her blog and in various shops in London. She has just won Food Writer of the Year at the Young British Foodie Awards, where judge Yotam Ottolenghi praised her 'jaw-droppingly foul mouth'. She is also studying for a PhD in Psychological Medicine. Follow Helen on Twitter @FoodStories. Or not. She does go on a bit …

Pedro 'El Malo' Ochoa Guzman was born in Sinaloa, Mexico, in 1977. The world's most unsuccessful drug trafficker, he is thought to be the only man ever to repeatedly cross the border the wrong way, resulting in the repatriation of an estimated $200 million worth of clinical-grade cocaine to Mexico. His efforts, blamed on bad tequila, earned him the Congressional Medal of Honor, and made him a figure of such derision among fellow traffickers that he was deemed too pointless even to shoot. He currently resides in Brownsville, Texas, where he leads an Elvis Presley/Dolly Parton tribute band.

Margot Henderson adopted London 30 years ago and has cooked her way round town since. Margot and her partner Melanie Arnold run the catering company Arnold & Henderson, as well as the fabulous Rochelle Canteen, famous for its delicious food, green grass and odd opening hours. It's often said to be one of London's best-kept secrets, hidden behind a brick wall with no sign. It's a treat to push open the door and discover this Shoreditch oasis. Margot is passionate about good produce and straightforward cooking.

Guys want to be him, girls want to be with him and children want to play with him. **Ben McFarland**, also known as the hairier half of the Thinking Drinkers, is a leading light on the beer-soaked literary landscape. He's been named Beer Writer of the Year not once, not twice, but on three different occasions – and his award-winning books include *World's Best Beers*, *Boutique Beer: 500 of the World's Finest Craft Brews* and *Good Beer Guide West Coast USA*, co-written with Tom Sandham – the other half of Thinking Drinkers. Not just a wordsmith of unprecedented prowess, he is also an international star of stage and screen. Together with Sandham, he has written and performed *The Thinking Drinker's Guide to Alcohol*, a comedy drinking experience which debuted at the 2011 Edinburgh Fringe and, following sell-out shows and excellent reviews, returned in 2012 and 2013 before transferring to London's West End. www.thinkingdrinkers.com

International barman **Sean Muldoon** is the founder and general manager of The Dead Rabbit Grocery and Grog. The Dead Rabbit is the culmination of Muldoon's lifelong dream to combine sophisticated cocktail service with the best of the Irish–British tavern tradition. Before this, he was at The Merchant Hotel in Belfast, which was declared 'World's Best Cocktail Bar' in 2010 at Tales of the Cocktail. Prior to his award-winning work at the Merchant, Muldoon ran his own business venture, The Perfect Drinks Company, a one-stop consultancy and event bartending service, which was the first of its kind in Ireland. **Jack McGarry** is The Dead Rabbit Grocery and Grog's bar manager, who also created its extensive historically based drinks programme. In July 2013, he was honoured with the prestigious Tales of the Cocktail International Bartender of the Year award. He is its youngest ever recipient, and only the second in America (after the legendary Audrey Saunders). Prior to joining The Dead Rabbit, McGarry tended bar at Milk & Honey, London, one of the world's most highly awarded bar operations. And before this, McGarry realised his bartending ambition of working with Dead Rabbit founder Sean Muldoon at The Merchant Hotel.

Daniel Bartholomew Crichton Pierre-Tate is the abbreviated pseudonym of notorious Indian charlatan Sunil Kumar 'The God' Parangarasa, currently on remand in Hyderabad for procuring one of a pair of boys from a sunny Kent milieu for the purpose of illicit paintings. Once billed as 'The Most Incredible Boy' at a live show where he produced a pistol and shot himself through the head, Pierre was thought to have gone forever; but he was soon reported in the company of Papoutsis and others, running an illegal souvlaki joint and brothel above the propshaft of a freighter. Sighted later in London, Mexico City, Holstebro, Berlin and County Leitrim, Ireland, where he was seen in the company of several sheep, Parangarasa is reputed to have been connected to a number of international intrigues, seemingly financed through novels of those same intrigues which are taken for fiction. In a statement from his cell in Hyderabad last year, Pierre said: 'I will give a hundred dollars to anyone who can send me a decent martini,' at which the prison complex was inundated with gin and vermouth from all corners of the globe, an event blamed for the notorious breakouts of both prisoners and guards which followed. He is thought to be at work on the book of those events, while he plots a live comeback, this time as 'The Mostly Acceptable Boy'.

José Pizarro trained as a chef in Cáceres, Extremadura, and moved to the award-winning Meson de Doña Filo in Madrid in 1997, where he fell in love with the fresh, brightly flavoured dishes of *nueva cocina*. He has lived in the UK for 15 years and in that time has worked at some of London's most prestigious Spanish restaurants, including Eyre Brothers, Gaudí and Brindisa, where he set up and ran the tapas bars. In June 2011 he opened his first solo venture to great critical acclaim – José, a tapas and sherry bar – followed by the award-winning Pizarro restaurant, a few yards from José. José is a regular on BBC1's *Saturday Kitchen* and an occasional contributor to food programmes on Channel 4 and UKTV, including Rick Stein's Spain series. He has authored two well-received cookbooks – *Seasonal Spanish Food* and *Spanish Flavours* – and was voted Trade Personality of the Year 2012 by *Harper's Magazine*.

Ross Shonhan's expertise in Japanese cuisine did not come through an obvious route: born and raised on a family-run cattle farm in Queensland, Australia, in 1997 he moved to Brisbane to serve rigorous apprenticeships at some of the city's top European and Oriental restaurants. In 2001, with five years of kitchen experience behind him, Ross moved to London to undertake a position as senior chef de partie at London's Asia de Cuba, before accepting a position as junior sous chef at The Dorchester Hotel. In 2005, he was recruited by the Nobu Group and appointed head chef at Nobu, Dallas. While opening the restaurant, Ross was personally trained by the acclaimed and highly influential chef and proprietor himself, Nobu Matsuhisa. Ross returned to London in 2007 having been headhunted by Rainer Becker's team for the role of head chef at Zuma. Adapting his traditional Japanese cooking methods to a more contemporary style, Ross defined the cuisine at Zuma, which soon came to be regarded as of one of London's finest restaurants. In 2012, the time came for Shonhan to open his own restaurant. The bustling streets of Soho proved to be the perfect setting for Bone Daddies Ramen Bar's shared benches and rock 'n' roll soundtrack. August 2013 marked the opening of his second restaurant, Flesh & Buns, in Covent Garden.

Torgren Torgrenssen was born near the Allied submarine base in Borgarnes, Iceland, in 1944. He is thought to be the product of a British submariner's tryst with a local girl, which ended with Torgren's abandonment after the war. We suspect this because his name is designed to seem Icelandic, but is not Icelandic, and nobody in Iceland has ever made sense of it. At infancy Torgren was threatened by a puffin. His hair turned snowy white, and he developed the nervous bowel which came to plague his later career as a crooner in the nightclubs of Borgarnes, where puffin increasingly graced the menu. As puffins proliferated he was eventually thrown out of the Borgarnes nightclub scene; there being only one club, it brought an abrupt end to his career. Fortunately, this 'opportunity in work clothes' prompted the travels informing his occasional self-published works on the famous objects and regions of the world, so that you might profit by his guidance, and avoid life's pitfalls by staying at home. As Torgren would say: 'Sit down.'

World-renowned messy eater **Andrew Weatherall**'s extraordinary twenty-five year career in music has been characterised by a series of unique partnerships, with 19 albums, 30 or so EPs and singles plus more than 250 remixes under his belt. Bastion of the underground, Andrew has set up record labels, remixed in collaboration with artists such as Paul Oakenfold on Happy Monday's 'Hallelujah', and has brought a distinctive flavour to hundreds of other artists. Remixes led to a smattering of production duties. Andrew very rarely wears the producer hat, but on each occasion he does, from Primal Scream's *Screamadelica* in 1991 to 2009's *Tarot Sport* by Fuck Buttons, the results are outstanding. In 2013, Andrew became Faber Social's inaugural Artist-in-Residence.

First published in 2014
by Faber & Faber Limited
Bloomsbury House, 74–77 Great Russell Street, London WC1B 3DA

Interior design by Faber & Faber
Additional design and layouts by Friederike Huber
Printed in Printed in China by C&C Offset Printing Co. Ltd

All rights reserved
© Yianni Papoutsis and Scott Collins, 2014

Photographs on pages:
7, 9, 10, 14, 16, 18, 21, 31, 32, 42, 44, 49, 50, 60, 65, 66, 68, 69, 70,
73, 75, 76, 88, 93, 95, 105, 112–13, 117, 119, 121, 123, 124, 127, 139, 141,
143, 148, 153, 156, 157, 160, 172–3, 178, 187, 190, 192, 194–5, 199, 200,
206, 208, 215, 216–17, 219, 221, 223, 226 © Paul Winch-Furness
22–3 © Ian Duff
41 © Scott's mum
197 © The Gaztronome
47 © Lynn Goldsmith/Corbis
175 © L. Saloni (cod), Smereka (udders), Soo Hee Kim (potatoes),
Optimarc (pie)/Shutterstock
144–5 © Randy Duchaine/Alamy
202–3 © Tristan Hutchinson/Millennium Images, UK
4, 34–5, 52–3, 57, 62–3, 78, 79, 80–1, 87, 96–7, 132–3 © Tom Bowles

Illustrations on pages:
vi, 3, 25, 37, 55, 83, 99, 131, 147, 183, 205 © DBC Pierre
100, 101, 224–5 © Shed
102–3 © Shed/I Love Dust
117 © I Love Dust

The right of Yianni Papoutsis and Scott Collins to be identified
as authors of this work has been asserted in accordance with
Section 77 of the Copyright, Designs and Patents Act 1988

A CIP record for this book is available from the British Library

ISBN 978–0–571–30299–4
Limited edition ISBN 978–0–571–30300–7

2 4 6 8 10 9 7 5 3 1